ESSENTIALS OF DIGITAL CONTENT MANAGEMENT & PRESERVATION

SANJEEV
Acting Librarian
Central University of South Bihar

Ess Ess Publications
New Delhi

ESSENTIALS OF DIGITAL CONTENT MANAGEMENT & PRESERVATION

ISBN: 978-81-934311-8-4

First Published 2018

Published by:
Ess Ess Publications
4831/24, Ansari Road,
Darya Ganj,
New Delhi-110 002.
INDIA
Phones: 23260807, 41563444
Fax: 41563334
E-mail: info@essessreference.com
www.essessreference.com

Cover Design by *Patch Creative Unit*

Printed and bound in India at Yash Printographics.

Dedicated to
MY PARENTS
&
FAMILY

Contents

Preface

This book is presented with a motive of developing a complete solution for librarians and information professionals for converting print documents in digital form. If we try to analyze the recent trend of information profession, we will find a countrywide feeling of creating digital versions of manuscripts, rare books, thesis and dissertations etc. available in print form in various libraries and information centers. Most of the professionals are involving themselves in these new tasks without having proper knowledge and expertise of the concept and initiating the process either by themselves or by outsourcing the whole process. Therefore, it is an appropriate time to provide a complete solution of digital preservation so that the library professionals may not only perform the process of digitization on their own but also may ensure the quality assurance over the technical issues of digital preservation. In this complete text, I have focused on all possible relevant theory and practice-based issues of digital preservation in the libraries.

Present book has been divided into seven chapters. The first chapter is "Sources of information", which discusses about various types of sources of information from documentary to non-documentary form. It also discusses on the history of recording information and papermaking. The second chapter is "Preservation and conservation". It provides complete information on the basic know-how on the preservation and conservation of library documents, various causes of deterioration of paper in the libraries and suggests various strategies for preserving them. At last, it discusses the digital preservation of library documents. It also enlightens the readers on the importance of specific policy for digital preservation in a library or information center. The third chapter is"Digitization basics". It comprehensively describes all of the technical issues relating to digitization activity. The fourth chapter is "Digitization tools". It presents information on the specific tools and information technology gadgets required for performing the process of digitization. It provides detailed information on various types of digital cameras and their functionalities. It also discusses on the accessories required while using or handling digital camera.The fifth chapter is on "Digitization process" and it deals with the complete process of digitization. It includes the information on the establishment of digitization laboratory, discusses minor but prominent activities for performing quality digitization processes, digitization standards and copyright issues. The sixth chapter is "Digital file formats", it discusses about the various types of formats of digital files and their suitability for specific type of document or information. At last, seventh chapter is "Digital file management system" and it primarily deals with various solutions of the digital file management system like DSpace, Green Stone Digital Library, FEDORA, etc. It also provides information on the Digital Curation, Web Archiving, evolution of digital preservation, security issues of Digital Right Management etc.

– Author

1

Preservation and Conservation

If we assess various fundamental characteristics of mankind, some of these are his capacity to generate culture, civilization and tradition, these are directly associated with the fact that it is possible for a man to distribute information not only at a personal or individual level but also within a society or over distances. He also holds the capacity to preserve such cultural issues over time. Modern tools of information technology have brought about quantum leaps to the world in many ways. It is evident that various civilizations, cultures have grown up in various parts of the world and later on ruined due to varied reasons in various epochs. The sources of information and storage media as we discussed in the previous chapter were made from very varied organic and inorganic substances like stone, clay, bark, papyrus, animal skin, and paper. In the inception the quantum of information was very less and the scholars were having a varied choice of information storage media. But it is found that they have chosen identical storage solution on the basis of the climatic, geographic condition and the availability of fauna and flora in their respective residential location. It is also identified that the interest of the scholars for recording information was to transmit them for next generations. And thus durability and preservation was the decision making issue while selecting the alternatives among various available information sources in the ancient era. In terms of the present demand of record keepers, librarians, archivists and curators for managing, keeping information sources of the past, one problem not only remains unsolved, the current solution is in fact worse than in the previous ages as how to store such archival records for long-term and also with the advent of information and communication technology, how to ensure easy accessibility of electronic documents. In fact there has been a negative development in this area over centuries.

PRESERVATION AND CONSERVATION

A number of organisations and writers have explained the term preservation in their own words. In all of these definitions the term is defined clearly for developing the understanding with this area of study. MacKenzie gives very broad definitions, which more or less cover the whole field of conservation (MacKenzie, 1996):

- preservation, in its current meaning in the archive world, refers to everything which contributes to the physical well-being of the collections;
- conservation, or direct physical intervention with the material, is only one part of preservation;
- indirect preservation includes the building, archive storage methods, security against threats, and handling;
- *preservation by substitution* or *reformatting*. This means making copies of the records, normally on microfilm, and then using the copies in place of the originals, thereby reducing wear and tear on the latter and preserving their condition.

The Memory of the World programme (Hoeven et al., 1996) refers this issue with the different terms, it is as follows:

- *preservation* is the organisation and programming of all kinds of activities regarding conservation of the collections in general;
- *conservation* is a concept that includes *preventive conservation* which aims to reduce the risk of deterioration: environmental control, regular maintenance and protection o f the collections by using appropriate treatment, anti-theft devices and creating surrogate documents for heavily-used original documents.

HISTORY OF PRESERVATION

Medieval documents on parchment have been shown to have been preserved for thousands of years. This was then replaced by rag paper – a medium whose durability is limited to centuries, followed by the acidic industrial paper of the 19th and 20th centuries which is a cause of much concern today due to its brittleness. Finally, in the digital age our information media are said to have a life expectancy of decades at the most, generally only of years. The long-term archival storage of electronic documents has become a problem which is only increased by the fact that it is generally met with indifference. Now a day the idea that today's knowledge overwrites yesterday's knowledge is prevailing. In the digital age, mankind is in the process of losing its historical dimension. It is an alarming development that has shook up the foundations of one of the central pillars of our culture.

The vary purpose of libraries, archives and other similar institutions is to preserve important documents with lasting scientific, artistic, or social value, so that future generations can access them just like we do today. Ancient sources require very costly preservation measures, these works printed on paper having an aggressive chemical content can be saved from destruction by storing them in microforms. Contrary to ancient techniques, Digital media is characterized by ideal properties with high longevity and agility.

> Bit streams images can be kept for long periods practically without loss of information. The sudden upsurge in the storage capacity of digital media permits to store enormous collections of extensive reference books on a DVD or Blu-ray discs. A single layered blu-ray disc can store up to 25GB of data. Compact storage devices i.e. pen drives with variant storage capacities are available in the market that facilitates mobility of data.

CAUSES OF DETERIORATION OF PAPER

All library materials are made up of organic matter whose degradation with the passage of time is a ecumenical phenomenon. Deterioration of paper-based object is essentially the perversion of cellulose. However, even fragile papers that are well handled could be durable (Akussah, 1991).

The major climatic reason of deterioration is the high temperature and relative humidity of the nature, this combination contributes greatly in accelerating the rate of various types of deterioration. If we try to examine various types of deterioration of paper, we will find following four categories of deterioration (Bankole, 2010):

Chemical deterioration : The prime reason of this category is natural ageing of the paper. A paper which is made up with the wood pulp sized with rosin in an acidic medium, becomes yellowish as the time passes; it also faces a rapid loss of original structure.

Mechanical deterioration : It is reflected through the

changes in the structure (like size and shape of the paper). It may be seen in the form of cracks, splitting and warping.

Incidental deterioration : It occurs due to accidents, this accident may take place due to any natural disaster like flood or fire, or any accident due to lack of proper handling of documents.

Biological deterioration : It happens when any living agent is involved in the degradation of library and archival material.

The causes of deterioration listed above could also be grouped into two types:

- Abiotic factor and
- Biotic factor

The first three causes constitute the abiotic factors while biological deterioration is caused by biotic or living agents. However, it is pertinent to point out that chemical, mechanical and biological agents act in co-associations, ranging from synergistic to antagonistic to deteriorate paper materials. The biotic factors stand as the most important cause of deterioration in tropical countries, due to the high ambient temperature and relative humidity that provide excellent condition for their proliferation and destructive ability (Bansa, 1981).

Further Bansa describes that the biological agents could be divided into two groups:

- Macro-organisms (those living agents that could be seen with the naked eyes and these include insects and rodents).
- Micro-organisms (the living agents that cannot be visualized with the naked eyes, but may be seen with the help of microscopes, and these include bacteria and fungi like moulds).

Biological Agents: Micro-organism- Moulds (fungi) and Bacteria

Mold is often used interchangeably with the word mildew. It is a generic terms that describes a variety of microorganisms, including fungi, algae, rusts, yeasts, and bacteria. All of these may work as agents of deterioration for paper based documents directly or indirectly. Fungi do not need energy from light for growth. The fungi bear microscopic spores that are produced in enormous quantities and are always present in the air. They are often water repellent and are resistant to desiccation (drying out). Extreme cold and hot climatic condition destroys them. The fungi grows on any organic material provided there is sufficient moisture fungal spores are found in both indoor and outdoor air samples, with the two main reservoirs being organic debris and soil (Domsch et al., 1980; Lugauskas and Krikstaponis, 2004). When the spores find favorable environment, they germinate. Moulds are opportunistic microorganisms of ubiquitous nature and the number of identified fungal (mould) species is well over one million (Mueller and Schmit, 2007). The conditions of favorable environment are different for each species. After landing on a host material, a spore requires sufficient moisture or humidity to germinate and find enough food. Mould spores, which are the means through which fungi are disseminated, are always present in the air, but sufficient moisture may remain in dormant state for long periods provided the environment is kept dry by maintenance of low relative humidity.

Cellulose-based materials, such as linen, paper and wood; and protein based material such as leather etc are particularly susceptible to direct attack by microorganisms. The presence of moulds on library collections is one of the important problems of acidic papers (Southwell, 2002). The factors that influence the fungal contamination of buildings and the level of contamination of books include installations and overall maintenance of premises, temperature, humidity, air circulation and the number of visitors (Godds et al., 1973; Lugauskas and Krikstaponis, 2004).

Age of print document is also a very important factor for their deteriorating the condition. Besides the extent of use and care during their use are few other issues of the concern in the context of deterioration. The availability of moisture is a prerequisite for biological decay to occur in paper materials, and it is a common observation that moisture alone causes significant reduction in the strength of papers. As such moulds proliferate in situations where conditions indoors are very moist, precisely when the relative humidity exceeds 70 per cent, which may arise from condensation of airborne water vapor on building surfaces or from leakage of water as a result of rain (Small, 2003).

It is observed that the higher relative humidity correlates with the high growth rate of mould. Wetting of collections which may arise for instance from water disasters increases susceptibility of papers to mould growth and makes conservation for the future problematic (Aziagba and Edet, 2008). In the stack areas of the libraries or in the location where we keep document at large, there is little air flow and the available air at such location is almost stagnant. Such conditions aggravate the mould contamination because it propagules of fungi in the air settle slowly on surfaces and start to grow (Lugauskas and Krikstaponis, 2004). For the growth of fungi, further nourishment is required. Dust is a major source of nourishment for fungi and even insects (Korpi et al., 1997). it could form a microenvironment on surfaces thereby hindering normal airflow over them, and the large surface areas of small dust particles could absorb moisture (Maggi et al., 2000). After observing the existence and growth of mould, it is essential to review the environmental condition; it will not only stop the further nourishment of mould or fungi but also control their growth.

Although mould is an important factor for deterioration of books, its exposure can also adversely affect on the health of the bookkeepers/library staff through these three processes: allergy, infection and by mycotoxin production (Singh, 2006). Most of the fungi may provoke immune responses in the form of diseases such as allergic rhinitis (sneezing attacks, nasal discharge or blockage), eye irritation, cough, bronchial asthma or hypersensitivity pneumonitits or farmer's lung depending on the nature of fungi, the dosage of exposure and the health status of the individuals (Pieckova and Jesenska, 1999; National Academy of Sciences, 2004). Nilsson et al. (2004) have observed that greater number of mould species in airborne dust samples from damp than in control residences with the major moulds being Aspergillus, Cladosporium and Penicillium. The residents of damp houses also had more complaints of allergic symptoms in the form of irritations of skin, eyes and respiratory tract. Meklin et al. (2002) and Cho et al. (2006) also reported the simmer issues.

Insects and rodents

Insects frequently cause extensive and often irreversible destruction of books in dark (nocturnal), humid, dirty and cluttered environments. Such environments provide ready food source where they can feed, lay eggs and pupate silently (Shuhaimi, 1986). The insects damage paper and other related objects through Termite, Silverfish, Cockroaches, Book lice, etc. Although termite is a very small, yellowish insect which primarily lives on wood, but if they damage books, they produce deep, crater-shaped holes, or deep, irregular erosions. At the time when termite starts damaging books, if the treatment is not done, this may lead to total destruction of the paper source. Silverfish is another insect it is wingless with long antennae. These are usually found in moist locations, normally under stones and boards, cracks or in dark places where humidity is more than 50%. Cockroaches are of reddish brown color. It is found in warm, damp and dark places like the bathroom, floors of kitchen, under the sink, near water pipes and cupboards. Booklice are small soft-bodied insects that have relatively large heads, fairly long antennae and strong-toothed mandibles.

Most of these insects can hide in cracks in bookshelves or inside books where the eggs settle in the gutter between pages. According to Ighinosa (2000) insects constitute the major problem to library development in Nigeria and that they do irreversible damage fast and secretly. Dike (1953) identified insects as the sole cause of deterioration of historical records, while Harris (1956) indicated that insects are the major factor in the deterioration of bibliographic records. Plumbe (1964) reported that tropical countries swarm with insects and pests, and that majority of the over 1,200 identified cockroaches were found in the tropics. Ighinosa (2000) noted that cockroaches are found in all libraries in the tropics and they bring about destruction of library materials in their insatiable demand for food. Termites are capable of devouring a whole library, and could do so rapidly and so complctcly than the librarian becomes aware. Wet or damp conditions of tropical countries create conducive atmosphere for termites, and the damage they cause are irreparable. Plumbe (1964) described Africa as the headquarters of termites. He suggests that the book pathology centre ought to be set up in several locations in the tropics where insects found on books could be promptly identified, and control measures proffered.

Rats, mice and squirrels eat and destroy adhesives and related materials in the library collection. They are attracted to confined dark places, and they cause much damage to collections that are infrequently handled before the destruction is noticed. The rodents could utilize library materials as food or they can soil and permanently disfigure the collections by urinating and defecating on them. Mice and rats also usually shred and chew paper materials to make nests. It is also pertinent to note that rodents' invasion of library materials could expose users to diseases (Bankole, 2010).

STRATEGIES OF PRESERVATION

Preservation is a highly technical process that involves proper planning along with implementation of strategies. Some of the strategies for preservation has been mentioned below:

Refreshing Data

Refreshing is the process of copying data from one medium to another of the same type. During the process of refreshment, the hope is that the bits of data do not change. The purpose of refreshment is to replace data in one medium with a copy that is sufficiently the same that the data can continue to be accessed without difficulty. For example, refreshment may consist of copying membership lists from an old floppy disk onto a CD-ROM disk so that the data can be accessed using the same database management software.

Refreshing is necessary because storage media deteriorate and the hardware needed to access and use data may change, meaning the storage media can no longer be used. For instance, people used to store documents on 3 ½″ floppy disks, but as computers stopped being manufactured with those disk drives, people had to copy the data onto other media, such as CDs or hard drives. The periodic need to refresh electronic records onto new media is inevitable given the continuous changes in computer storage media. However, selecting the best media available can reduce the frequency for refreshing data, since high-quality and stable storage media should remain usable for a longer period.

Records professionals are advised not to 'jump on the bandwagon' of new media technologies too quickly, since the media chosen may not in fact be sustainable in the long term.

For example, 'zip drives' became popular in the mid-1990s because the disks provided greater storage capacity than the floppy disks commonly used at the time. By 2004, however, sales had decreased considerably, as more and more people used CD-ROM and DVD technologies. Computer manufacturers stopped building computers with zip drives, and it became harder to access the storage media. Today, CDs and DVDs are popular and common storage devices but it is always possible a new technology will replace them, in which case it will be necessary to refresh the data by moving everything to a newer storage medium.

While refreshing is not supposed to involve changing the software used to read the data, it is often necessary not just to refresh data but also to migrate data to new systems, in order to make it accessible with new computer programs. Migration is discussed below.

Whenever data is refreshed, the files that have been moved should be verified at the bit level by completing a checksum or other verification or validation process, as described later in this module. This validation process is intended to ensure that the content has been copied without corruption or loss.

Replicating Data

Replication is a similar process to refreshment, but with one difference: the location where the record is stored will likely be different when a file is replicated. Again, the goal of replication is to ensure the bits of data do not change. Data that exist in only one location are highly vulnerable to damage or loss. The software or hardware could fail; someone could alter or delete the files accidentally or intentionally; or the data could be lost in a fire, flood or other environmental disaster. Replication helps ensure the survival of information, by storing the files in several different locations.

Replication is different from refreshing data, since the new copy of the electronic record is stored in a different place. Replication is also different from the process of backing up data, since replication may involve copying specific electronic records, whereas backup processes usually involve copying entire systems, with software and data together. Accessing replicated files requires knowing what software and hardware were used to create the records in the first place, which makes the preservation of metadata so important.

Migration

In order to access old or archived documents with upgraded software *migration* or on a new computer, most experienced computer users have already *everywhere* migrated tons of documents. This is not the only reason for migration: the Internet connects an enormous variety of computer generations of different makes, each with their own individual hard- and software configurations. Whenever Internet users want to exchange documents, they have to find a means – most often by applying migration – to make the documents readable for their partners. An often cited definition of migration was given in the final report of the Task Force on Archiving of Digital Information (TFADI 1996):

Migration is the periodic transfer of digital materials from one hardware/software configuration to another or from one generation of computer technology to a subsequent generation. The purpose of migration is to preserve the integrity of digital objects and to retain the ability for clients to retrieve, display, and otherwise use them in the face of constantly changing technology.

Hendley (1998) has analyzed a large number of document categories and their corresponding data formats. Below table lists the major results naming current standards. For some documents containing data of a single type only, a few well-established standards exist. Two particularly successful formats for the visual representation of texts and graphics are PDF and PostScript. For compound documents (i.e., documents containing data of different types), standard data formats are still missing. In this field, which among others includes virtual reality systems, Office applications, and geographic information systems, proprietary formats flourish. Some of these systems offer export filters to open up ways for data exchange (Jones and Beagrie 2001). As long as there are no standard formats for a compound document type, a document's components have to be exported separately.

Migration in Long-Term Preservation

Migration in the strict sense transports and digital document from some old platform onto a new platform. There is a natural differentiation between hardware and software transfers, as well as between approaches that result in changes of the data holding devices, the data formats, or the logical data structure. At first, we concentrate on the potential *target data formats* of a migration, especially focusing on long-lasting standards. Independent of the strategy used for long-term preservation, metadata have to be kept permanently readable.

DIGITAL PRESERVATION

The concept preservation of digital resources presents challenge at both technical and organizational level, and many challenges remain to be fully resolved. However, these difficulties should not be seen as obstacles in establishing practical preservation policies. The term 'digital preservation' is used to refer to the overall approach to preserving information and records created using computers, including electronic records.

Definition

According to the Cornell University Library (2000:2003) the goal of digital preservation is to maintain the ability to display, retrieve, and use digital collections in the face of rapidly changing technological and organizational infrastructures and elements.

Issues to be addressed in digital preservation include:

- Retaining the physical reliability of the image files, accompanying metadata, scripts, and programs (e.g., make sure that the storage medium is reliable with back-ups, maintain the necessary hardware and software infrastructure to store and provide access to the collection).
- Ensuring continued usability of the digital image collection (e.g., maintain an up-to-date user interface, enable users to retrieve and manipulate information to meet their information needs)
- Maintaining collection security (e.g., implement strategies to control unauthorized alteration to the collection, develop and maintain a rights management program for fee-based services)

Although this section is one of the last of the tutorial, issues associated with longevity need to be discussed at the onset of any imaging initiative. Many of the issues that become impediments to long-term preservation are rooted in early decisions centering on selection and conversion. Digital preservation decisions and strategies should be developed as an integral part of a digital imaging initiative as many decisions will be closely coupled with an institution's long-term retention plans.

DIGITAL PRESERVATION POLICY

At this juncture we have decided to preserve library resources. In the process of preserving library documents a specifically focusing towards their digital preservation, it is essential to develop a strategy for taking sincere initiatives. We can also perform all of these activities in the form of a project with a specific time schedule. During the course of digital preservation we are bound to take decision on diverse issues relating or affecting the process of digital preservation. We can take these decisions separately or at the movement of their necessity and the process of digital preservation will not suffer directly. But this type of compulsive initiation will not present a holistic approach and may affect in long run. Therefore it is suggested to develop and implement a Digital Preservation Policy duly approved by Library Committee or governing board of parent organization. In this policy librarian should try to incorporate all those issues relating to selection of documents for digital preservation, technologically gadgets, manpower, legal issues, quality control and standards etc.

BENEFITS OF DIGITAL PRESERVATION POLICY

Major benefits of implementing Digital Preservation Policy are as follows:

- To develop a digital preservation strategy
- To plan coherent digital preservation programs
- To ensure and reinforce accountability
- To demonstrate that such funds can and will be used responsibly and consistently
- To ensure digital materials available for current and future use
- To define the significant properties that need to be preserved for particular classes resources
- To assist agencies in designing digitization programs

- To provide a comprehensive statement on the digital preservation
- To provide security measures that ensure the protection of digital materials during us

A digital preservation policy could guarantee many benefits at each institutional level, such as ensuring digital materials available for current and future use, providing a comprehensive statement on this theme and planning coherent digital preservation programs. Besides, the formulation of a policy allows to deal with difficult subjects as the short-lasting life span and small capacities of digital materials, the obsolescence of the hardware required to access them, the obsolescence of software for reading the data and file formats and, finally, the structural and technical heterogeneity of the different types of digital materials.

In according to an institution's achievable resources, the main scope of a digital preservation policy is to achieve the following objectives:

- preserving and providing continued access to digital material, both born digital and digitized material;
- ensuring that preserved digital materials are authentic;
- preserving damage and deterioration of the physical media of pickles by ensuring an environmental control.
- reversing damage, if it's possible;
- changing the format of digital materials to preserve their intellectual content, if it's necessary.

The basic requirements of Digital Preservation Policy are as follows:

- Legal requirements
- Financial requirements
- Business requirements
- Technical requirements
- Maintenance procedures

- Preservation strategies
- Technology forecasting
- Historical value

The reasons behind the positioning of policy development for digital preservation within institutions are several and can vary according to the specific juridical and institutional contexts; in many cases, the political context in which a policy is formed weights heavily as well as the legal environment. Moreover, there are other relevant factors, such as the substantial financial requirements, the business requirements to take evidence of decisions and activities and ensure the historical value of digital materials. Technical requirements constitute another important reason for developing a policy, specifically as far as it concerns the definition of technology forecasting, maintenance procedures and, especially, preservation strategies, or rather the precise guidelines for reformatting, refreshing, migrating, emulating and bundling data to newer technological platforms.

STRAINS IN DIGITAL PRESERVATION

It is the demand of time to preserve digital documents in the libraries and archives. Although various initiatives have been taken by various organizations and funding agencies, but a number of obstacles are creating hurdles in the process. Various difficulties in the implementation of digital preservation based initiatives can be grouped into following two categories:

- Technical
- Organizational and Administrative

Technical issues

In this category we have identified some issues related to the technology and the process, specifically software, hardware, operating system, their capabilities and limitations. These issues are:

- It is difficult to identify an appropriate storage media. During this process of identification, it is essential to check the possibility of physical deterioration, mishandling, improper storage, and obsolescence of that storage media.
- Due to obsolescence or over-reliance on any proprietary and unsupported file and compression formats we can face problems in future. So, the adopted file format must have all qualities for ensuring the satisfaction of library user and it should support library system in terms of space, processing, retrieval and dissemination.
- The implemented system should ensure the integrity of the files. Further it should safeguard the content, context, fixity, references, and provenance.
- The technological gadgets which are not directly related with the digitization process or digital preservation may also effect the whole system in terms of storage and processing devices, general or library programs, operating system, interfaces of digital access and network or other protocols.
- As we are living in the era of resource sharing, compatibility is having prime importance in the information access and delivery culture. Therefore, it is essential to examine the status of compatibility of adopted applications with the popular software solutions. The systems which are accessible through web are more concerned with this issue.

Organizational and Administrative issues

In this category we are discussing on the issues related to the organizational setup, man power, expertise and willingness. These issues are:

- It is identified that there is an insufficient institutional commitment for long-term preservation

- In the absence of preservation policies and procedures, it becomes difficult to ensure consistency for the same.
- In the developing countries scarcity of human and financial resources is creating hurdles in taking initiatives.
- The lack of interest of stockholder in creating and maintaining digital repository.
- A tendency of switching over the system is identified among young generation staff. It negatively effects the initiation, will power and continuity of developing such digital repository.
- Inadequate support of record keeping and limited administrative metadata also presents obstacles in achieving the target.
- The definition and description of copyright and fair-use of information/documents is not sufficiently popularize among the librarians community, which creates a feeling of fear and finally stops enthusiastic librarians in taking initiatives.

STRATEGIE FOR DIGITAL PRESERVATION

For ensuring digital preservation of Digital documents, we may taking various initiatives which may be clubbed together in the following strategies:

Technical strategies

Enduring Care should be seen as an ongoing strategy for monitoring the wellbeing of digital resources. Vigilant management of the collection includes housing images and accompanying files in secure, reliable media and locations; storing and handling media according to industry guidelines to optimize their life expectancy; and implementing periodic and systematic integrity checks and backups. Refreshing involves copying content from one storage medium to another. As such it targets only media obsolescence and is not a full-service preservation strategy. An example of refreshing is copying a group of files from CD-ROMs to DVDs. Refreshing should be seen as an integral part of an enduring care policy.

Migration is the process of transferring digital information from one hardware and software setting to another or from one computer generation to subsequent generations. For example, moving files from an HP-based system to a SUN-based system involves accommodating the difference in the two operating environments. Migration can also be format-based, to move image files from an obsolete file format or to increase their functionality.

Emulation involves the re-creation of the technical environment required to view and use a digital collection. This is achieved by maintaining information about the hardware and software requirements so that the system can be reengineered.

Technology Preservation is based on preserving the technical environment that runs the system, including software and hardware such as operating systems, original application software, media drives, and the like. Digital Archeology includes methods and procedures to rescue content from damaged media or from obsolete or damaged hardware and software environments.

Organizational strategies

Technical solutions alone are insufficient to ensure the longevity of digital resources. A holistic approach is called for that recognizes the interdependencies between technical and organizational components. Among issues to be addressed in such a strategy are staffing and training needs, financial requirements, criteria for re-selection, and preservation metadata needs.

Although it is useful to examine each issue in detail, successful solutions require the integration of administrative and technical considerations. For example, an institution may have a well-developed strategy for day-to-day maintenance of image collections that codifies how to monitor, test, and refresh files. However, unless there is a concomitant financial and administrative plan that outlines how to staff and finance these activities over time, the maintenance plan may not succeed in the long-term. Likewise, having dedicated and qualified staff will not suffice unless there is a technical appreciation for the lifecycle management of digital assets. Effective management of digital collections will require institutions to develop and follow a business plan for evaluating long-term preservation and access requirements, identifying costs and benefits, and assessing risks.

Examples of initiatives that support such an approach include:

- **Arts and Humanities Data Service (AHDS)** in the UK is developing a decision-making tree to be used in cost-benefit analysis of digital preservation options (Administrative and Managerial Frameworks Preservation Management of Digital Materials).
- **Cornell's Risk Management of Digital Information project** examined the risks involved in file format migration (e.g., TIFF 4.0 to TIFF 6.0) and developed an assessment tool to evaluate the risks involved in migration. This tool also helps to assess institutional readiness for any digital preservation action.

The following initiatives are examples of promising, practical approaches to digital preservation:

OAIS (Open Archival Information System) reference model provides a framework for long-term digital preservation and access, including terminology and concepts for describing and comparing archival architectures. Both the NEDLIB and Cedars 1 projects have adopted the OAIS reference model as a basis for their explorations.

Pieckova, E. and Jesenska, Z. (1999), "Microscopic fungi in domestic dwellings and their health implications in humans", Annals of Agriculture and Environmental Medicine, Vol. 6, pp. 1-11.

National Library of Australia (2004), "Preservation policy", available at: www.nla.gov.au/policy/ pres.html (accessed 10 December 2007).

Nilsson, A., Kihlstrom, E., Lagesson, V., Wessen, B., Szponar, B., Larsson, L. and Tagesson, C. (2004), "Microorganisms and volatile organic compounds in airborne dust from damp residences", Indoor Air, Vol. 14, pp. 74-82.

Meklin, T., Husman, T., Vepsa¨la¨inen, A. et al. (2002), "Indoor air microbes and respiratory symptoms of children in moisture damaged and reference schools", Indoor Air, Vol. 12, pp. 175-83.

Cho, S., Reponen, T., LeMasters, G., et al. (2006), "Mold damage in homes and wheezing in infants", Annals of Allergy, Asthma and Immunology, Vol. 97 No. 4, pp. 539-45.

IARC (1993), "Some naturally occurring substances: food items and constituents, heterocyclic amines and mycotoxins", IARC Monographs on Evaluation of Carcinogenic Risk to Humans, International Agency for Research on Cancer 56, Lyon.

Gong, Y.Y., Cardwell, K.K., Hounsa, A., Eggal, S., Turner, P.C., Hall, A.J. and Wild, C.P. (2002), "Dietary aflatoxin exposure and impaired growth in young children from Benin and Togo: a cross-sectional study", British Medical Journal, Vol. 325, pp. 20-1.

Kelman, B.J., Robbins, C.A., Swenson, L.J. and Hardin, B.D. (2004), "Risk from inhaled mycotoxins in indoor office and residential environment", International Journal of Toxicology, Vol. 23, pp. 3-10.

Aziagba, P.C. and Edet, G.T. (2008), "Disaster-control planning for academic libraries in West Africa", The Journal of Academic Librarianship, Vol. 34 No. 3, pp. 265-8.

Shuhaimi, H. (1986), "The effects of environmental factors on library and archival materials and services", Environmental Information, p. 5.

Ighinosa, I.O. (2000), "Insect control in libraries: a case study of cockroaches in the tropics", Nigerian Libraries, Vol. 34, pp. 64-9.

Dike, K. (1953), Report on the Preservation and Administration of Historical Records and Establishment of Public Record Office in Lagos, Government Printer, Lagos.

Harris, J. (1956), "Notes on book preservation inWest Africa", Walas News, Vol. 2, pp. 1-25.

Plumbe, W.J. (1964), The Preservation of Books in Tropical and Subtropical Countries, Oxford University Press, London.

TFADI (1996), TFADI: Preserving digital information - final report. Task Force on Archiving of Digital Information. http://www.rlg.org/ArchTF (1996).

Hendley, T (1998), Comparison of methods and costs of digital preservation. *British Library Research and Innovation Report 106* (CimTech Ltd, University of Hertfordshire 1998).

Jones and Beagrie (2001), *Preservation Management of Digital Materials: A Handbook* (The British Library, UK 2001). http://www.jisc.ac.uk/dner/preservation/ workbook/

Digital Preservation Policy. http://www.iccu.sbn.it/PDF/normative_it.pdf

2
Digitization Process

PROCESS OF DIGITIZATION

Now it is clear that digitization is an exciting preservation option while providing unparalleled access available to all. The technology is advancing rapidly and this raises the question of accepted standards for digital preservation technology. The standards for image capture, resolution, data transfer protocols, indexing, access, and file types must be of sincere consideration. Some of the important considerations are as follows:

Defining your requirements

The first consideration before even thinking about equipment is to define the end use of the images. On this will depend what resolution of images and what file sizes are required, and hence the equipment and time scales involved. It is also essential to consider how you will store and access the scanned images and to ensure that your budget includes the cost of the right software to meet your requirements.

Choose the right equipment

It is important to remember that scanning technology

advances quickly and enhancements are regularly incorporated into new products meaning hardware has a high depreciation rate and may quickly become obsolete and uneconomical to maintain.

The main types of capture devices available are:

SCANNERS

These are most common and traditional tool for converting print document to digital documents. A wide range and variety of scanners are available in the market, which may be choose on the basis of the features of the documents. Some of the types are:

High end A3 flatbed scanners

These are suitable for all types of photographs, transparencies, negatives and pages up to A3 size that may be laid absolutely flat. They are best used to produce files of 20 Mbyte plus. They are not suitable for bound volumes, glass plates, mounted slides, formats larger than A3 or, because they use very bright light, anything that is in danger of fading.

Source : **Website of kenrockwell (2011)**

Hand Scanners

A Hand scanner is a hand held manual device which is dragged on the surface of the image to be scanned. This type of scanner requires a steady hand, to avoid uneven scanning rate/speed that may produce distorted images.

Source : **Homepage of largescanner (2011)**

Drum Scanners

These are used by reprographic houses. Whilst they produce very high quality results they are expensive and the originals have to be fastened around a drum, which means they need to be very flexible and unmounted.

Source : **Homepage of scanmaster (2011)**

Medium format scanning backs

Scanning backs are essentially the devices that convert a medium format conventional camera into a hi resolution camera. With the right accessories, they are ideal for capturing items that cannot be placed on a scanner.

Pen Scanner

This type of scanner is used in the form of normal writing pen or highlighter. User is required to place the scanner on the target text and perform dragging. This type of scanner is used to scan written text.

MM scanners

These would seem to be ideal for collections made up of slides only. However, many of them are aimed at the domestic market and will not be robust enough for any reasonable sized collection. They often struggle to produce up to 18 Megabyte files of a good dpi.

Source : **http:// uk.shopping.com (Accessed on 03-11-2011)**

DIGITAL CAMERAS

Digital cameras come in a variety of standards. To be suitable for digitization work these must be of a professional standard and capable of 18 Megabytes plus, with interchangeable lenses and accessories.

Source : **Website of newdigital photography (2011)**

WORKSTATIONS

All capture devices will need a dedicated workstation of good specification and with monitors capable of proper calibration, appropriate scanning software, a CD writer and the ability to store a reasonable number of images, either on the hard drive or server.

SETYING UP A SCANNING LABORATORY

Before digitization can start there are a number of things needed to consider. Over and above the environment needed to run computers the following are essential:

- A stable power supply - fluctuations can ruin scans and make consistency impossible.
- The scanning equipment must be installed in a proper clean area - dust and dirt is exaggerated when viewed on-screen.
- The workstation must be co-located with the scanner - The person who digitize, must be able to view the scan on–screen while working.
- Check links to networks or servers are available - you will be moving large files.
- If cameras are used the ambient light should be fully controllable - overhead lighting or the variability of daylight will add a permanent color cast and make consistency impossible.
- The studio should have solid floor to prevent vibration - no digitizing is instantaneous.
- There must be sufficient room and suitable surfaces to clean items, handle and store them before, during and after scanning.
- The area must be secure.

DECISIONS ON PROCEDURES RELETING TO DIGITIZATION

Although the major part of the complete digitization process is image capturing, but being information professional, it is equally important to maintain the originality of print document, incorporate documentation based support for ensuring its easy retrieval and also to make digital document sufficient enough for achieving the best possible user satisfaction. For ensuring these issues, we should consider following things during the complete process of digitization:

Sorting and Cataloguing

Every item to be digitized must be clearly identifiable. If the digital file name is not marked or labeled on the original item, then it should carry some other unique identifier, such as an accession number, which can be associated with the file name during the scanning process.

Job Specification

Before starting the work, the rules and conventions must be decided for the job. For example:

- What file type and final size or resolution is required?
- Should monochrome prints be captured as RGB or greyscale. Should images to be rotated for upright orientation?
- Should operators crop to edge of item or inside edge of print/negative? It should be specified whether captions are to be included if they are located outside the regular cropping convention, or exclude all or some types of captions.
- Should color casts to be corrected? Film transparencies and negatives very often have a color cast created by the film material, lighting conditions or processing - or a combination of all three. There are methods for

detecting the presence of and correcting such irregularities.

- Is re-touching to be done? If so, to what extent, at what screen size and what is the maximum time to be spent on each item?
- Is the original unprocessed scan to be retained?
- If visible or digital watermarks are to be applied - to which resolution versions and when in the process?

Prepare your materials

Before scanning you need to prepare your equipment and originals for final handling and processing.

Batching

Where possible group original items in batches of same size/ format materials, say 100 - 150 in a batch. This will make the work easier to manage and improve productivity. It also means quality issues can be more easily isolated and corrected.

ICC Profile Checking

Ensure the monitors are all calibrated and profiled to the same standard, that the capture devices are individually profiled and that the final files are all tagged with the required device independent ICC color profile.

Pre-cleaning

If materials have been in storage for any length of time a degree of controlled cleaning may be desirable. Cleaning processes should be carried out well away from the digitization area using lint free cotton and surgical gloves.

Oil mounting

Oil mounting is a specialist technique that can significantly reduce effect of scratches, ground in dirt and other damage to negatives or transparencies.

Adjust and check your scans

This is an important step and often overlooked in the planning. Once the image is captured it must have basic checks carried out, either immediately after capture or in batches at a later time.

Color range and balance

Check that the capture device's sample range has been utilized and neither end of the tonal. If color cast correction is to be carried out, this is the time to do it.

Cropping and rotating

Carry out cropping as decided in your job specification and, if necessary, rotate the image for correct orientation.

Re-touching

Carry out re-touching to the standard decided in the job specification - this needs training and/or experience. Retouching on photographic image will always show if not done to a professional standard.

Compression

Where required create a compressed version of the image.

Multi-pack creation

Where required create screen resolution multi-pack versions.

Water-marking

Where required apply visible or digital watermarking to specified versions of the image.

Quality inspection

It is advisable for a quality inspection of say 20% of output to be carried out by a qualified person who hasn't been involved in either scanning or post-processing.

Ideal Steps of digitization

Ideally a digitization process should involve following steps:

1. Image preparation;
2. Preparation of the volumes, issues and pages of the document for scanning;
3. Scanning pages of the document;
4. Editing images of the document;
5. Using Optical Character Recognition Software (OCR) on images to edit text versions. (OCR is the process whereby a computer program "reads" the text from an image of a document and converts it into ASCII text);
6. Creating a searchable database of the text; linking text to images;
7. Mounting on Web.

Image preparation

The first step is to take all measures that are necessary to preserve the hard copy of the documents. A physical review of the document revealed much variance in the condition of the pages and that, while some could withstand scanning without any preservation, other pages would not. Consultation took place with the preservation library assistant in the rare book section at the university library and procedures were set up to follow:

1. Trim each page so that no rough edges are left;
2. Mend rips and tears with acid-free binding tape;
3. Put each issue in an acid-free envelope and store each volume in an acid-free storage box.

Important factors to consider for format

At this stage it is necessary to decide the most appropriate file format for the online version of the document. The integrity of each page had to be maintained and in order to do this, save the pages after scanning as images. There are two primary options:

1. Save the image as a PDF (Portable Document Format) file using Adobe Acrobat;
2. Save the image as a GIF (Graphical Interchange Format) or JPEG (Joint Photographic Experts Group) file.

It is investigated to save the images as JPEG files, which would be most appropriate. JPEG will allow the entire project to be uploaded as an HTML file and furthermore, JPEG retains more information as it compresses an image:

- Each page had to be kept intact so that the user could view the page online just as it appeared in the paper copy;
- User-friendliness was important. Therefore, the online version had to be searchable, had to have a minimum of side-to-side scrolling, had to load fairly quickly and the pages had to be clear and easy to read;
- Optical Character Recognition (OCR) would work on scanned images of the document. This was a consideration as several different fonts were very small and that cannot always be recognized by OCR programs;
- With standardization the maximum number of users should be able to view it.

Scan pages of the document

Having determined the type of file to be used for the online version, several preliminary scans were conducted to determine the appropriate image type, brightness, contrast, height and width, as well as the length of time it would take for each page to be scanned. To ensure uniformity in scanning the following parameters have been investigated for set up:

Height: 12.65 in.

Width: 8.18 in.

Brightness: 125 (approx.)

Contrast: 130 (approx.)

Image Type: Black and White Photo

File Type: JPEG

Image Quality: 600 dpi

The selection process for identifying specific documents for digitization anticipates all the major steps/ stages of whole project implementation. The end quality of produced digital documents not only depends on the nature and importance of the original sources but also it depends on the nature and quality of the digitization process. Further it is equally important that how carefully the relevant information is captured from the original print source and later on organized, indexed, disseminated to users and finally maintained over time.

For taking a decision on to the selection of documents, these are presented in a sequence that moves from relatively abstract assessments of intellectual value to nuts-and-bolts issues concerning whether available resources and technology can provide a product that meets expectations. In practice, the pieces interact in ways that are often complex. Decisions about what to digitize must first and foremost address the intellectual value of the original sources. We are likely to be able to convert only a small percentage of existing scholarly materials to electronic form, and doing even this will require substantial investments. We therefore need to determine what it is truly worthwhile to convert. Some scholarly resources are heavily used; others are consulted infrequently. With only limited funds available for reformatting, types and levels of use can help to shape priorities.

A person reading a book, looking at a photograph, or consulting a manuscript encounters few barriers to use. One might have to handle an object carefully, or use a magnifying glass to read fine print, but in general the work is immediately approachable. The same resource, when digitized, should be equally accessible and approachable. Ideally, the electronic version will also permit new kinds of use and more sophisticated types of analysis.

Decisions to digitize must take into account the physical size, nature, and condition of source materials as they affect the characteristics of the desired product. They must likewise address whether available means of conversion can satisfy expectations for the result. Projects must also, from the very first, consider how users will be guided through the electronic version.

After an extensive analysis of the above mentioned issues it is sorted out that a librarian or an information officer should consider following points while planning for the digitization of documents in his library and information centre:

Assessment of scholarly value of Library material

Materials with marginal scholarly value are best left in their original form or made accessible in a less costly manner. Scholarly value, of course, is a subjective assessment and even the most marginal materials can support some kinds of research. Most users, nonetheless, would opt for electronic access to original monographs rather than to derivative works, or to the papers of a prominent scholar over the administrative records of a university department. Bibliographers regularly make purchase decisions that reflect their evaluation of the intellectual quality of single items or collections of materials. Similar judgments apply in choosing what to digitize.

Digitization and the intellectual value of the digital material

Scholarship can be facilitated when texts are made fully searchable by rekeying (retyping) them or by employing OCR software. Comparisons between successive drafts of a text and the final published work, for example, or with later editions and translations, are vastly simplified when the words and phrases are searchable. A concordance or thesaurus is likewise most easily mined when it is in searchable form. Electronic texts can be moved readily from one environment to another (from the World Wide Web onto the hard drive of a personal computer, and then into a word processing program, for example), shared with other users, and manipulated and reconfigured for multiple purposes. Digitized prints, drawings, and other visual resources can be viewed in groups at low resolution or inspected individually for very fine detail. Digital charts and tables, appropriately coded, can be loaded directly into statistical software packages for additional analysis.

Electronic accessibility of body of information of original books, manuscripts, photographs, or paintings A collection of thousands of portrait images, however promising a resource, might be nearly unapproachable because of its size and the condition and dimensions of individual items. Well-indexed and in digitized form, however, the collection could be searched with relative ease for images of a particular person or for some indexed characteristic (the country from which the portrait originates, for example). Likewise, the digitization of large-format architectural drawings could enable comparisons of small- and large-scale drawings, different views of the same architectural feature, or sequential phases of construction.

Increased value of the combination or aggregation of original sources increases their value

Digitizing related scholarly monographs, like building a coherent collection of paper copies, can strengthen the context within which each title is approached. Ephemera-leaflets from a political campaign, for example-are often most useful when studied in the aggregate, as are posters, broadsides, and popular literature. Harvard has digitized da gu erreotypes fro m thirte en re po sitories to fa cilitate the combinations and comparisons that are otherwise precluded by the fragility, value, and dispersion of the original images.

Popularity of digitized source material which is being consulted among scholars

Intensive use does not automatically make a collection a good candidate for digitizing. If the primary audience is local, for example, and if competition for a particular resource is not a problem, access may already be sufficient. Ephemera produced by a community political organization may be of great interest to local scholars and of limited value to a worldwide audience. On the other hand, if use is heavy and widespread, digitizing may at once guarantee convenient and reliable access, and make it possible for some institutions to discard their original copies. The JSTOR project, through which a large array of core scholarly journals is being made accessible in digital form, is a prime example of an initiative focusing on high-use materials.

Digitization may provide wider access

Low use may signal that a collection has marginal intellectual value, but there are many other reasons for valuable materials to have generated little interest. A collection may be held in a remote location, for example, or be owned by an institution with highly restrictive access policies. Bibliographic records may be poor, as is often the case with pamphlets. The value of digitizing such materials may go beyond the simple fact that the resulting files can be widely distributed. Broader access, as it creates a new community of users, can also facilitate more active scholarship.

Physical condition of the original materials limit their use

Some resources are too fragile to be consulted. Aging newspapers or palm-leaf manuscripts that break at the slightest flex simply cannot be browsed. In such cases, a digital copy might be provided to improve access, and a microfilm or other photographic surrogate made to ensure long-term survival. (Film can be made from a digital file or vice versa.)

Sources may also be at risk because of high user demand or extraordinary monetary value

A nation's founding documents, glass-plate negatives of vanished architectural sites, or rare maps may benefit from the creation of digital copies that satisfy the purposes of most users. These files do not necessarily need to meet archival standards. They are created to protect the originals from handling.

Related materials are so widely dispersed that they cannot be studied in context

Cooperative efforts to digitize disparate pieces of a greater whole can create or restore a more usable collection. Papyrus fragments, a prominent individual's far-flung correspondence, scattered photographs of a particular subject or by a specific photographer and broken serial runs are among the many materials whose coherence, accessibility, and scholarly utility can be enhanced through digitization.

Manageable size and format of Digital files

Digital resources need to match users' technical capabilities and equipment. Most require Internet access and standard web browsers, or a CD-ROM drive. Images delivered to the Internet in formats other than JPEG or GIF require additional software for viewing or printing. Even when electronic resources are optimized for on- screen delivery, some network connections, particularly those via modem, are still far too slow to support browsing of digital collections at satisfactory speeds. And scholars in some locations may lack training opportunities or the ongoing technical support needed to take advantage of the electronic environment. These limitations, however, are not necessarily reasons to rule out digitizing. The worldwide trend is toward greater capabilities. Moreover, the more important the resources available electronically, the greater the incentive to acquire the network, viewing, and printing technology necessary to use those resources. Digitization may, in and of itself, stimulate improved access.

Digitization and the needs of local students and scholars

Immediate demand can inject a measure of practical reality into decisions to create electronic resources. A historian may choose to teach from digitized images of manuscripts that would otherwise be unavailable to a large class. Because ready access to shared electronic files can transform the classroom, proposals to digitize in support of immediate teaching needs may garner faculty support.

Various approaches of Digitization and its facilitation to a researcher

Different digitizing techniques result in electronic files with different characteristics. These in turn can correspond well or poorly with scholarly needs. If the goal is to provide an image based finding aid that helps users identify original materials of interest, for example, m ou nting slo w-lo a ding hig h-re so lu tio n im a ge s wo u ld be counterproductive. If, on the other hand, the intention is to reduce or eliminate handling of original materials, an image that fails to convey all critical information embodied in the original will fail to serve its intended purpose.

The simplest approach to digitizing involves use of a scanner or digital camera to create electronic pictures (bitmap images) of original materials. Decisions concerning the number of dots recorded by the scanner (resolution), how many shades of gray or colors will be recorded (bit depth), and other factors related to scanning equipment and settings will determine how well the digital product replicates the original. High-quality bitmap images can usually capture all the significant detail in texts or graphics. Scanning rare and unique texts or visual resources can make them accessible to users who would otherwise never see them. In such a case, merely reproducing the original in electronic form represents an extraordinary enhancement.

For textual materials, post-scan processing can support expanded capabilities

Scanned text can be processed with Optical Character Recognition software to produce searchable indexes. OCR software is now only occasionally employed in digitizing projects because it cannot yet interpret accurately all fonts and alphabets, and because it adds significantly to per-page costs. Text can also be rekeyed to create ASCII files-very straightforward digital text files that permit searching by keywords or phrases. In some cases this enhancement is the primary justification for digitization. Directories, dictionaries, and indexes are all significantly easier to use when specific words can be searched within a well-designed digital file.

ASCII texts accommodate key-word searching (e.g., searching for all instances of the word "temperance") and some kinds of analysis, but they do not readily replicate the structure and format of an original document. Without special coding, researchers cannot directly consult the seventh paragraph of the third chapter of a particular text. Nor can they search for all occurrences of "welcome" used as a verb rather than a noun. These capabilities become possible in marked-up texts, which are coded to highlight elements of structure, format, and syntax. The Standard Generalized Markup Language (SGML) is the emerging model. One SGML application, the Encoded Archival Description (EAD), is being used to create electronic versions of archival finding aids.

These and other approaches to digitizing carry very different costs, benefits, and resource requirements. While electronic versions can be more versatile than original materials, in some cases they hinder research. A scholar studying bookbinding or papermaking, for example, is poorly served by a reproduction of any kind. So too is the scholar whose immediate access to a large and important collection of literary works is sacrificed in order to serve a worldwide constituency-perhaps because bound volumes have been disbound for scanning.

Digitization increase the utility of the source materials

Digitization can enhance original materials in many ways. Image quality can be improved by eliminating extraneous stains and marks. Thumbnail images of visual resources (photographs, drawings, and paintings) can be browsed to discover patterns, trends, and relationships among individual items, and specific images can then be scrutinized at higher resolution. Likewise, patrons can review scanned images to identify needed materials before requesting that they be retrieved from storage.

Electronic transcriptions of texts, in ASCII format or marked- up files can be linked to bitmap images of original documents. Readers can then decide for themselves whether "authoritative" transcriptions are in fact accurate. Comparisons of different versions of a text are likewise simplified. Related texts and images can be assembled together within a single, unified corpus. Examples such as the Geet Govind project of UNDP, administered by Indira Gandhi National Centre for Arts, New Delhi is an interactive, multimedia document on Archaic and Classical India, suggest the potential of electronic texts.

Almost all electronic products will provide basic links that allow users to navigate them (to locate a particular map within a printed text, for example). The degree to which a digitization project exploits electronic links will depend upon its intended use. For digital resources created as pedagogical tools, predetermined connections are part of the package. Products intended for research tend to be less aggressive in ordaining relationships among sources, since their creators assume that researchers will build their own structures of meaning.

Critical features of the source material must be captured in the digital product

The cost and nature of digitizing hardware and software continue to evolve, and preferred solutions are likely to shift as well. It may sometimes make sense to defer certain digitizing projects so that technology can catch up to needs. The success of a project to digitize oversized maps at Columbia University, for example, depended partly on the ability of users to see detail and read place names. As a result, the maps were scanned at relatively high resolution, thereby creating challenges for digital image delivery and presentation. File sizes were very large and initially outran the capacity of the library's computers and network. Greater bandwidth and more powerful machines have enhanced functionality.

Digitization process retained source material

Automatic sheet feeders are fast and efficient, but they may destroy brittle paper. Digital cameras can minimize the manipulation of source materials, but subjecting certain media-watercolors, for example prolonged lighting is problematic.

Issues of hardware which is used for conversion

Color slides, for instance, cannot be fully represented by scanners that create only black-and-white images. Even a color scanner with limited capacity to reproduce tonalities will be inadequate when high-quality images are important. Digitizing equipment can be expensive, and the costs may be difficult to justify when use is sporadic. Some projects may thus be done most economically if they are contracted out. Agreements with external vendors, in addition to specifying technical conditions, performance expectations, and handling guidelines, must fully define ownership and distribution rights for all digital products.

Digitization of information resources which continue to grow ongoing commitments and extended arrangements for copyrights may be required when collections are still expanding, as is the case with current journals and annual reports, or the papers of a living individual. Consultations with scholars and other experts can be particularly useful, since the long-term value of current materials is often difficult to discern.

Users navigation within and among digital collections

Printed sources orient readers by means of tables of contents, chapters and sections, pagination, indexing, and formatting cues. Manuscript materials often rely on finding aids linked to the organization of file folders. Photographs may be mounted in albums. At a minimum, electronic products need to provide the same kind of functionality. The process may require several steps. For a multi- volume work that has been scanned page by page, for instance, each page is a separate computer file that must be individually labeled and stored. The files for critical pages of the work-for example, the title page, table of contents, and the first page of every new chapter-must then be linked to electronic navigational tools so that they can be easily located.

Existence of Digital files in the Information Centers

Bibliographic records, finding aids and indexes can all be adapted to include references to electronic resources. Nonetheless, our ability to determine what has been digitized remains well behind what we know about materials that have been microfilmed or photocopied.

One of the principal challenges is to determine what information is essential in describing an electronic product. The "Dublin Core" and other special initiatives for structuring and standardizing descriptive data propose to combine information about the technical characteristics of digital files, their location, and a summary of their contents. The resulting records are known as "metadata." Their function is to provide users with a standardized means for intellectual access to digitized materials. Despite these and other initiatives, projects to catalog digital files are only in the developmental stage. No system has yet been widely adopted for tracking the digitizing activities of libraries, although new approaches continue to emerge.

Better delivery of Digital products to users

Alternative modes of digital storage and delivery must be considered from the outset of a project. CD-ROMs, for instance, are distributed and used differently from information made accessible over the Internet. The differences are reflected in hardware requirements, software, and ease of use. CD-ROMs are sometimes bundled with software for searching and analysis that is superior to that generally provided for Internet files. On the other hand, access to CD-ROMs is limited to individual workstations or small networks, while Internet files can be made available to a very broad audience. And Internet resources, by nature, can be updated or augmented without requiring users to replace objects that have become obsolete.

Internet products, however, generate questions of their own. How immediate must access be?

Files can be mounted on a server so that they are instantaneously available on-line. They can be stored on disks in a jukebox and loaded on demand ("near-line" access), or kept off-site ("off-line") and retrieved and delivered on demand. Near-line and off-line access can save on server space and requirements, though there are countervailing staff costs associated with retrieving and mounting the files. Expected demand, file sizes, fee structures, and available staffing and equipment must all be considered.

Authorization of use of the digital resources and required circumstances

Copyright holders may limit distribution rights, institutions may be unable or unwilling to provide the infrastructure needed to support universal access, and cost-recovery enterprises cannot by definition make their products available without restriction. Digitizing projects must thus consider access policies and control, pricing mechanisms, and billing procedures. Access issues impinge upon selection decisions in a number of ways. A university may mount high-resolution images of unique holdings for scholarly use (a medieval manuscript, an important collection of drawings), but would not allow unauthorized publication of those images. Moreover, electronic resources cost money that must be secured through subsidies or fees. When neither internal budgets nor external subventions provide adequate financial support, digitization will require a paying audience.

Access, when it is not universal, must be managed

Current alternatives include passwords, direct user fees, and limitations according to organizational affiliation. Different capabilities for viewing, downloading, and printing may be offered at different prices or to different sets of users. There are many options, each reflecting a different pathway toward a self-sustaining endeavor.

Ensure the integrity of the digitized data

The malleability of electronic products makes them particularly useful for many kinds of scholarship. Digitized files must be embedded with detailed information concerning the methods used to create them. The same information should be included in external bibliographic or descriptive records. Users who are consulting or copying the sources must also be able to confirm that the files they see or receive match the originals. Means to authenticate and protect digital products, long available in financial and industrial applications, are only beginning to take hold in the scholarly world.

Adequacy of the existing technology infrastructure to fulfill local demands

Robust computer systems and an appropriate number of work stations are perhaps more easily provided than such ancillary features as network printing capabilities in the library and in offices, classrooms, and residences.

The Goal of the project is to long-term preservation of deteriorated materials

Preserving documentary resources in electronic format presumes that, to the greatest extent possible, all the information contained in the original material has been captured completely and accurately. This requires careful attention to significant detail, whether the smallest text characters on a page or all the shades and tones of blue and green in a seascape. Targets for resolution, grayscale, and rendition of color either exists or is being developed to ensure the needed detail and fidelity.

Digital preservation also requires a supporting organization and infrastructure dedicated to storing the electronic files and to migrating them to new formats and/ or media as technology change. Unless these capacities are all in place, digital files cannot be regarded as permanent. Creating an enduring digital preservation master file is a multidimensional task with long-term implications. Hybrid projects, in which digital files are complemented by copies on microfilm, alkaline paper, or some other stable medium, provide the insurance that exclusively electronic projects do not.

Availability of already digitized source material

As we have seen, it can be difficult to determine whether a specific item has been digitized and by what means. If an electronic copy does exist, is it accurate, satisfactorily functional, and accessible? Does it take advantage of the capabilities of current technologies? If the existing product does not serve the intended purposes of the proposed project, a new version may be warranted.

Benefited User Group of the proposed digital product

It is important to consider whether the product will support better teaching or research and enable students to learn more, or in different ways-if, for example, texts or images are more fully revealed. Digitization may allow librarians to manage collections and provide services more effectively, or to provide traditional services such as copying or interlibrary loan at lower cost or at less risk to collections.

Commensuration of the intellectual value of the proposed product with the expense

The limited resources available for digitization might have greater impact if they were directed at another project, or directed toward an entirely different approach to providing access-through exhaustive indexing perhaps, or microfilming, or some other type of reformatting that would prove in the end more useful to scholars.

Creation of acceptable digital product at lower cost

When materials are scanned to support short-term course work, for example, careful (and expensive) post-scan processing to eliminate extraneous marks and speckles or to deskew misaligned images may be a waste of time. Likewise, an adequate substitute for full-text scanning of little-used journals might be provided by linking scanned tables of contents and indexes to bibliographic records and relying on traditional forms of document delivery.

How will the proposed project address the long-term costs associated with digital files?

The accumulated body of digital products may enable savings elsewhere in the institution-for example, by reducing staff costs for reshelving bound journals, or by lowering the costs of storage, circulation, and preservation-and these savings could offset some or all of the expense of digitizing. But such savings as may be realized are difficult to predict. It is essential to realize that the costs of digitization are just beginning at the time of initial capture. The programmatic capacity to distribute and maintain electronic resources, and to migrate them to new forms as original digital platforms fail and formats and software are superseded, is fundamental to long- term efforts. In addition, there are staff costs associated with training and user support. Finally, rising user expectations may require that existing digital files be reprocessed in new ways. When OCR software is perfected, for example, unsearchable bitmap images of texts could be thought unsatisfactory. Projects that do not plan for change may become obsolete, and therefore irrelevant.

Research libraries are eagerly embracing the digital world

They are acquiring access to great quantities of electronic materials produced outside their walls. At the same time it becomes essential to maintain digital versions of all worthwhile existing text material of their own holdings. A careful review, analysis, and planning can yield electronic resources that are functional and faithful to the original sources, and that support new kinds of scholarship. A detailed plan of work, regular assessment of progress, closely documented adjustments and corrections, and the retention of other project-related data can strengthen the knowledge base for future efforts.

QUALITY ASSURANCE

While performing digitization work, It is essential that all digitization work undergoes a series of quality control analyses at each and every stage. Regardless the digitization work is done by in- house unit of the library or the assignment is outsourced. Before initiating the process we should identify the standards and specifications of various regulatory agencies/authorities. Bearing in mind limits on time and finances, some form of sampling may be necessary to reduce the costs of this process, as with the NARA who state that at a minimum 10 images or 10% of images (whichever number is higher) need to undergo quality control (these should be selected randomly from the entire collection) (Lee, 1999). Lee further mentions that the Ideally Quality Assurance (or QA) must be performed on all master images and their derivatives with each step being fully documented. The types of things one should look for are:

- size of image
- resolution of image
- file format
- image mode is correct (i.e. colour images are in colour, not greyscale)
- bit depth
- details in highlights and shadows
- tonal values
- brightness
- contrast
- sharpness
- interference
- orientation
- noise
- alignment of colour channels
- cropped and border areas, missing text, page numbers, etc.
- alignment of image (i.e. excessive skewing that is not the result of the such things as the tight binding of a book)
- missing lines or pixels
- dithering
- poor quality interpolation with access and thumbnails
- text legibility

The overall return should be checked for file name integrity, completeness of job, and overall meeting of digitization project scope. NARA recommend that if more than 1% of images looked at fail the above quality control checks then the job needs to be redone. The Library of Congress concurs with many of these findings. For the American Memory Project running under the NDLP

(National Digital Library Program) it established a fifteen-point workflow practice for the Quality Review stage covering such areas:

- Verify delivery of 100 percent of files
- Inspect 10 percent of file contents
- Ensure technical requirements have been met
- Provide feedback to contractor
- Review any re-work

Aids and more specific guidelines to help in the testing of such ideas as contrasts and noise are available with accepted test cards and procedures. A good place to start to look for these is the Photographic and Imaging Manufacturer's Association/IT10 Still Picture Imaging web page has a growing list of standards.

DIGITIZATION STANDARDS

In the world of globalization of economy and resource sharing among libraries, it is imperative to follow international standards especially in a process which is going to develop a user oriented service. In an area related to information technology, any recommendations made now would most probably be redundant in a year's time with the changing capabilities of the capture devices, software, and falling prices. Therefore, before starting the process of digitization we should explore various updated guidelines of some prominent federal agencies or voluntary organizations.

Specifications

According to Lee, the specifications suggested for any digitization project will be variable for all the reasons outlined throughout this book. At the outset, however, projects should derive a set of standards which will allow full informational capture of the originals, following accepted practice in benchmarking. Having done this, there may need to be accommodations made to take account of available resources. The standards should not just specify requirements for the archival master, but should also state the parameters for the derived products:

High resolution (Archiving resolution) used for highest quality digitization (e.g. Oxford's Celtic and Medieval Manuscript project), for archiving file format with 'full informational capture', for outputting to high-quality print and film surrogates (in the case of graphics/text documents). The distinction between preservation copies and preservation quality images should be noted.

With graphics one of the most important factors is resolution. Different resolutions are required for different purposes, with high resolution often equating to an increase in unit costs. Furthermore, the digitization industry at present is awash with various projects digitizing at different resolution levels, and there are no archival or access standards available to which everyone adheres. Take for example a picture of a map. The digitizer scans the picture in at 600 dpi (e.g. a 5" x 4" print, with the image of the map filling the whole photograph exactly). However, if the original map was in fact 25 inches across (i.e. five times the width of the picture) the 'effective dpi' would be 600/5, i.e. 120dpi. Franziska Frey notes that 'a growing consensus within the preservation community is that a number of image files must be created for every photograph to meet a range of uses' (Lee,1999).

COPYRIGHT ISSUES

There are many interdependent and interacting factors to be weighed in selecting materials to digitize. The specific choices that result from the selection process will reflect subjective judgments, any of which may change over time. Nuance assessments, ambiguity, and shades of gray are all to be expected.

Questions concerning copyright, however, are far more clear- cut. Simply stated, if a proposed digitization work involves materials in the public domain, the work can proceed. If the source materials are protected by copyright but rights are held by the institution or appropriate permissions can be secured, the work can move ahead. If permissions are not forthcoming for copyrighted sources, however, the materials cannot be reproduced. Copyright assessments thus play a defining role with regard to digitization projects.

Copyright issues in the digital environment are still very much in flux and have provoked ongoing international discussion. While the broad thrust of digital technology is toward enhanced access, diminished costs, and more versatile capabilities, it is far less clear that copyright law will likewise encourage wider use. The legal strictures applicable to a particular project will vary depending on the country in which the project is based, the country in which the source materials were produced, and prevailing international agreements. Different kinds of materials, moreover, usually pose different types of rights-management issues. The performance rights associated with musical scores, for example, or exhibition rights for films, differ from rights for nonperformance materials such as electronic journals or documentary photographs. To complicate matters, all these rights are susceptible to change over time.

Digital projects must be undertaken with a full understanding of ownership rights, which is difficult as they often are to ascertain, and with full recognition that permissions are essential to convert materials that are not in the public domain. Rights that must be negotiated with the copyright holder often entail fees. The institution hosting a project may also have policies and procedures that inform intellectual property negotiations. The legal office of most institutions can provide guidance. The Internet site IFLA: Copyright and Intellectual Property Resources is a good resource for maintaining current awareness. It includes articles, reports and white papers, discussions, and information about organizations related to copyright issues, intellectual property in general, and electronic distribution of intellectual property.

REFERENCES

http://kenrockwell.com (Accessed on 03-11-2011)

http://www.prepresstech.com/used_prepress _ equipment/howtek/howtek_scanmaster_4500.html (Accessed on 03-11-2011)

http:// largescanner.net (Accessed on 03-11-2011)

http:// newdigitalphotographytips.com (Accessed on 03-11-2011)

http:// uk.shopping.com (Accessed on 03-11-2011)

3
Digitization Tools

The term photography is derived from the greek word. Sir John Herschel was the first person who used the term "Photography". In the year 1839 the process of photography became publicly popular. Photography is a process which involves two distinct scientific processes. These scientific processes are related to the capturing and storing of images.

PINHOLE CAMERA

A pinhole camera, also known as camera obscura, or "dark chamber", is a simple optical imaging device in the shape of a closed box or chamber. In one of its sides is a small hole which, via the rectilinear propagation of light, creates an image of the outside space on the opposite side of the box

In case of Pinhole camera, Images created via a small opening will be found in the natural environment and in everyday life. This type is very popular in various parts of the world since ancient period. Probably the earliest surviving description of this kind of observation dates from the 5th century BC, written by Chinese philosopher Mo Ti. In the Western hemisphere, Aristotle in 4 BC was asking, without receiving any satisfactory answer, why sunlight passing through quadrilaterals. In 10 AD the Arabian physicist and mathematician Ibn al-Haitham, known as Alhazen, studied the reverse image formed by a tiny hole and indicated the rectilinear propagation of light. There was another scholar during the Middle Ages who was familiar with the principle of the camera obscura, namely the English monk, philosopher and scientist Roger Bacon. It was not until the manuscript Codex atlanticus (c. 1485) that the first detailed description of the pinhole camera was set down by Italian artist and inventor Leonardo da Vinci, who used it to study perspective.

***Source*: website instruction tables (2011)**

Pinhole camera is a smaller version of that room, and the film inside the camera replaces human memory. The film records the image through the pinhole. The pinhole forces every point emitting light in the scene to form a small point on the film, so the image is crisp. The reason a normal camera uses a lens rather than a pinhole is because the lens creates a much larger hole through which light can make it onto the film, due to which the film is exposed faster. The photographer exposes the film for a long time because the pinhole lets so little light through. In the pinhole camera the pinhole acts as the lens.

TWIN-LENS REFLEX (TLR) CAMERAS

Double-lens cameras seem first to have been developed around 1870, when it was realized that having a second lens alongside the taking lens meant that one could focus without having to keep swapping a ground glass screen for the plate afterwards, making the time delay in actually taking the shot rather less(1). This sort of approach was still used as late as the 1960s, as the monstrous Koni-Omegaflex testifies. A twin-lens reflex camera (TLR) is a type of camera with two objective lenses of the same focal length. One of the lenses is the photographic objective or "taking lens" (the lens that takes the picture), while the other is used for the viewfinder system, which is usually viewed from above at waist level. Besides fulfilling the basic objective, the viewfinder consists of a 45-degree mirror (that is why the word reflex is in the name), a matte focusing screen at the top of the camera, and a pop-up hood surrounding it.

Source : **website of sheldonbrown (2011)**

Higher-end Twin Lens Reflex (TLR) Camera may have a pop-up magnifying glass to assist the user in focusing the camera. In addition, many have a "sports finder" consisting of a square hole punched in the back of the pop-up hood, and a knock-out in the front. A photographer can sight through these instead of using the matte screen. This is especially useful in tracking moving subjects since the image on the matte screen is reversed left-to-right.

Many TLRs used front and back cut-outs in the hinged top hood to provide a quick-action finder for sports and action photography. Late model Rollei Rolleiflex TLRs introduced the widely- copied additional feature of a second-mirror "sports finder". When the hinged front hood knock-out is moved to the sports finder position a secondary mirror swings down over the view screen to reflect the image to a secondary magnifier on the back of the hood, just below the direct view cutout. This permits precise focusing while using the sports finder feature. The magnified central image is reversed both top-to-bottom and left-to-right. Due to this feature, Rolleis has become the leading choice of press photographers during 1940s to 1960s.

The typical TLR is medium format, using 120 roll film with square 6×6 cm images. Presently, only the Chinese Seagull Camera is still in production, but in the past, many manufacturers made them. The Ciro-flex produced by Ciro Cameras Inc. rose dramatically in popularity due in large part to the inability to obtain the German Rollei TLRs during World War II. The Ciro-flex was widely accessible, inexpensive, and produced high quality images. Models with the Mamiya, Minolta and Yashica brands are common on the used-camera market, and many other companies made TLRs that are now classics. The Mamiya C series TLRs had interchangeable lenses, allowing focal lengths from 55mm (wide angle) to 250mm (telephoto) to be used. The bellows focusing of these models also allowed extreme close-ups to be taken, something difficult or impossible with most TLRs. The simple, sturdy construction of many TLRs means they have tended to endure the years well. Many low-end cameras used cheap shutters however, and the slow speeds on these often stick or are inaccurate.

There were smaller TLR models, using 127 roll film with square 4×4 cm images, most famous the "Baby" Rolleiflex and the Yashica 44. The TLR design was also popular in the 1950s for inexpensive fixed focus cameras such as the Kodak Duaflex and Argus 75. Though most used medium format film, a few 35mm TLRs were made, the Contaflex TLR being the most elaborate, with interchangeable lenses and removable backs.

The smallest general-use TLR camera is the Swiss-made Tessina, using perforated 35mm film forming images of 14×21 mm. It has been argued that the "business end" of the Olympus Gastro Camera is technically the smallest actual TLR device.

SINGLE-LENS REFLEX (SLR) CAMERA

Digital single-lens reflex (SLR) cameras are the standard tool for professional photographers. With the introduction of cameras such as the Nikon D40/D40x (current entry-level model is the Nikon D3000) and the Canon Digital Rebel XTi (current entry-level model is the Canon Rebel T3), the market for digital SLR cameras has expanded tremendously. A point-and-shoot compact digital camera can offer reasonably good image quality, but a digital SLR, which usually looks a lot like an old standard 35mm film camera and may use the same lenses, offers the various advantages including:

- Accurate, large, and bright optical viewfinder.
- Fast operation and fast controls.
- Excellent image quality in low light situations when it is necessary to use higher ISO speeds.

- Interchangeable lenses

The single lens reflex (SLR) cameras are serious camera, in these cameras same lens is used for viewing and for taking photographs. A mirror in the body directs the light from the lens up into a prism for viewing, and then flips up out of the way just before an exposure is made. Professional photographer's or standard photo journalist's Nikon from the 1960s or 1970s was an SLR camera with a roll of 35mm film behind the mirror. When the mirror came up the light passed through to the shutter, which opened to expose one frame of film for perhaps 1/60th of a second. A Canon Digital Rebel or Nikon D80 looks very similar and works in almost the same way. The only difference is that instead of a piece of film behind the shutter there is an electronic sensor.

The mirror and optical view finder are what enable a photographer to frame images more quickly and accurately than with a point-and-shoot camera. Regardless of what lens or filters photographer has attached to the camera he/she see what the sensor will see. The typical digital SLR camera viewfinder offers additional information underneath the image, including all the most important camera settings.

Source : **website 3dmodelfree (2011)**

A digital SLR may offer the same number of megapixels, individual image elements, as a high-end point-and-shoot. Not all pixels are created equal, however. Resolution is important if you intend to make large prints but dynamic range, the ability to capture detail within bright highlights and dark shadows, is more critical in many situations. The sensors in digital SLRs are typically much larger than those found in point-and-shoot cameras. The main advantage of a larger sensor is better performance in dim light. If there are 8 megapixels spread out over a sensor that is 4 times larger than the sensor in a point-and-shoot camera that means more photons of light will fall on any given pixel. If during an exposure 50 photons would fall on the small sensor then 200 photons would fall on the big sensor. If there is a small change in the light from one part of the scene to another the sensor in the point and shoot camera is trying to notice a single extra photon; the electronics in the camera with the big sensor have four extra photons that are much easier to detect.

There are three kinds of digital SLR systems being made as of September 2005:

- Big lenses, big sensor
- Big lenses, small sensor
- Small lenses, small sensor

BIG LENSES, BIG SENSOR

Canon and Kodak have taken the most obvious approach to the challenge of transitioning from film to digital: build a digital sensor exactly the same size as one frame of 35mm film. The result is a chunk of silicon 24x36mm in size, which is vast compared to the sensor in a point-and-shoot digicam. The benefit of this vast sensor is reduced noise, which looks like grain, in low light/high-ISO situations. The drawback of a vast sensor is that manufacturing a flawless piece of silicon this big is very expensive. Consumer-priced cameras in this category include: Canon EOS 5D, Canon EOS 5D Mark II, Nikon D700, Nikon D3 and Sony Alpha A900. If one has a strong back and an unlimited budget, the Canon EOS 1Ds Mark III is a great choice. It is probably the best digital camera made and produces image quality that rivals medium format film (e.g., 6x6cm Hasselblad). The only other full-frame digital SLRs made were the discontinued Kodak DCS Pro SLR/n and SLR/c bodies.

BIG LENSES, SMALL SENSOR

Most of the digital Single Lens Reflux cameras fall into this category. The front part of the body use to have same lens mount. The back part of the camera has a sensor which is moderately smaller than 24x36mm standard frame. Due to this new design, the camera looks like an old film camera but it multiplies the magnification with the help of new and modified lenses. One does not require capturing the complete information on the extreme left and right, similarly extreme top and bottom of the frame. For capturing in digital file, what we see optically is more essential and thus viewfinder is provided for making required adjustments. If the photographer belongs to the moving film photography, he may feel difficulty and do require to some fresh mental and psychological adjustments. A 50 mm normal lens on a big lens/small sensor camera use to behave like a 80 mm tele-photo lens in a film camera. A 20 mm ultra wide angle lens use to behave like a 30-32 mm little bit wider angle lens on a film camera. Normally most of the popular digital SLR cameras belong to this category.

SMALL LENSES, SMALL SENSOR

The biggest problem with the "big lens, small sensor" situation is that photographers are forced to cart around lenses that are much larger, heavier, and, theoretically, more expensive, than they need to be. This has led to the introduction of lenses that have the big lens mount for a 35mm film camera but optically cover only the small sensor of a mid-range digital SLR. These are sold as "digital-only lenses" or "digital camera lenses" but in fact they won't work on a full-frame digital SLR. (Greenspun, 1997)

CAMERA LENS

The camera lens is an invention that attempts to duplicate the operation of the human eye. Just like the eye, the lens sees an image, focuses it, and transmits its colors, sharpness, and brightness through the camera to the photographic film, which, like our memory, records the image for processing and future use. Lenses are made of optical glass or plastic. They focus light rays by refracting or bending them so that they meet or converge at a common point. A simple lens "sees" well through its center, but its vision around the edges tends to blur. Blurring, color changes, distortion of lines, and color halos around objects are caused by defects in the lens called aberrations. Some aberrations can be corrected in the simple lens by shaping one or both surfaces so they are aspheric; aspheric curves vary like the curves of a parabola, rather than staying constant like the curvature of a sphere. A camera lens reduces the effects of aberrations by replacing a simple lens with a group of lenses called lens elements, which are lenses of different shapes and distances of separation.

The lens becomes more complex as greater correction of vision is achieved. The lens will also be more complex depending on the size of the aperture, the opening that allows light to pass through and the range of angles it "sees". Lens design used to rely on the optician's art and considerable experimentation. Now-a-days computer programs can adjust the shaping and spacing of lens elements, determine their effects on each other, and evaluate costs of lens production.

Lens elements are usually described by their shape. The convex lens curves outward; a biconvex lens curves outward on both sides, and a plano-convex lens is flat on one side and outwardly curved on the other. There are also concave lenses, biconcave, and plano-concave lenses. The elements are not necessarily symmetrical and can curve more on one side than the other. Thickening the middle of the lens relative to its edges causes light rays to converge or focus. Lenses with thick edges and thin middles make light rays disperse. A complex camera lens contains a number of elements specially grouped. The combination of the composition, shape, and grouping of the elements maximizes the light-bending properties of the individual elements to produce the desired image. The lens is focused by moving it nearer or farther from the film or focal plane. The lens can be twisted, causing the lens elements to move in and out along a spiral screw thread machined into the casing of the lens. Twisting the lens also moves a scale on the casing that shows the distance of the best focus.

The stop or diaphragm is a specialized part of the lens. In simple cameras, the stop is a fixed stop or a ring of black sheet metal that is permanently set in front of the lens. Box cameras, studio cameras, and some cameras of European manufacture use a sliding stop, which is a strip of metal that slides across the front of the lens between grooves. It has two or more holes of different sizes that are the apertures. Lenses with a variable stop have a machined ring on the outside of the lens mount, printed with f-stop numbers. By turning this ring, the diaphragm can be opened or closed. This iris diaphragm works much like the iris of the eye in allowing adjustments for varied light conditions.

The lens in a compact camera is usually a general-purpose lens with a normal focal length that takes pictures of an image the way our eyes see it. Lenses designed for special purposes are used with more advanced cameras.

Telephoto lenses work like binoculars or telescopes, and make a distant image appear closer. Wide-angle lenses make the image appear farther away; a panoramic lens is a special kind of wide-angle lens that is useful for taking pictures of broad expanses of scenery. Some disposable cameras are equipped with panoramic lenses. A fish-eye lens is also a special kind of wide- angle lens that deliberately distorts the image so the central part is enlarged and the outer image details are compressed. Fish-eye lenses cover very wide angles like horizon-to-horizon views. Another special purpose lens is the variable-focus lens, also called a "zoom" lens. It uses moveable lens elements to adjust the focal length to zoom closer to or farther away from the subject. These lenses are complex and may contain 12 to 20 lens elements; however, one variable-focus lens may replace several other lenses. Some compact cameras also have limited zoom, telephoto, or wide-angle features.

The lens of the camera evolved from optical lenses developed for other purposes, and matured with the camera and photographic film. In 1568, a Venetian nobleman, Daniel Barbaro, placed a lens over the hole in a camera box and studied sharpness of image and focus. His first lens was from an old man's convex spectacles. The astronomer Johann Kepler elaborated on Barbaro's experiments in 1611 by describing single and compound lenses, explaining image reversal, and enlarging images by grouping convex and concave lenses.

During 1800s, the first box cameras had a lens mounted in the opening in the box. The lens inverted the image on a light-sensitive plate at the back of the box. There was no shutter to open the lens; instead, a lens cap was removed for several seconds or longer to expose the plate. Improvements in the sensitivity of the plate necessitated ways of controlling the exposure. Masks with different sized openings were made for insertion near the lens. The iris diaphragm was also developed to control the aperture. Its metal leaves open and close together to form a circular opening that can be varied in diameter.

In 1841, Joseph Petzval of Vienna designed a portrait lens with a fast aperture. Previously, lenses made for daguerreotype cameras were best suited for landscape photography. Petzval's lens allowed portraits to be taken ten times faster, and the photograph was less likely to be blurred. In 1902, Paul Rudolph developed the Zeiss Tessar lens, considered the most popular ever created. In 1918, he produced the Plasmat lens, which may be the finest camera lens ever made. Rudolph was followed shortly by Max Berek, who designed sharp, fast lenses that were ideal for miniature cameras. Other essential developments in lens history include lens coating technology, use of rare-earth glass, and calculation methods made possible by the computer. Katharine B. Blodgett developed techniques for thin-coating lenses with soap film to remove reflection and improve light transmission in 1939. C. Hawley Cartwright continued Blodgett's work by using coatings of metallic fluorides, including evaporated magnesium and calcium that were four-one-millionths of an inch thick.

Design of a camera lens begins by identifying the user of the camera. Being a user based product, it is essential to identify the market or various types of user groups. With its identification, we can a camera designer may identify following issues:

- Specifications of the technology
- Design of external body
- Expected requirements of the output
- Due to technological advancements, a number of technological solutions are available. It is the requirement of user, which gives us support/blueprint in customizing the new product for the market.

The lens designer selects the optical and mechanical materials, the optical design, the appropriate method for making the mechanical parts, and, for auto focus lenses, the type of inter-face between the lens and camera. There are conventions or patterns for the different categories of lenses, including macro, wide-angle, and telephoto lenses, so some design aspects are standardized.

The group of lenses is called lens elements, which are of different shapes and distances of separation, make up the camera lens. Lens design used to rely on the optician's art and considerable experimentation. Today, computer programs can adjust the shaping and spacing of lens elements, determine their effects on each other, and evaluate costs of lens production. In selecting materials, the engineer must consider a range of metals for the components and various types of glasses and plastics for the lenses etc. When the designer completes the design, its performance is tested by computer simulation. Computer programs that are specific to lens manufacturers tell the designer what kind of image or picture the lens will produce at the center of the image and at its edges for the range of lens operation. Assuming the lens passes the computer simulation test, the criteria for performance that were chosen initially are reviewed again to confirm that the lens meets the needs identified. A prototype is manufactured to test actual performance. The lens is tested under varying temperature and environmental conditions, at every aperture position, and at every focal length for zoom lenses. Target charts in a laboratory are photographed, as are field conditions of varying light and shadow. Some lenses are aged rapidly in laboratory tests to check their durability.

After completing this process, additional design work is needed if the lens focuses automatically, because the auto focus (AF) module must work with a range of camera bodies. The AF module requires both software and mechanical design. Extensive prototype testing is performed on these lenses because of their complex functions and because the software is fine-tuned to each lens. For developing the complete set of lenses, the specific raw material including the lenses themselves, the coating, the barrel, or housing for the camera lens, and lens mounts are essential.

MANUFACTURING PROCESS OF CAMERA LENSES

Optical glass is supplied normally provided by lens manufacturer in the form of a "pressed plate" or sliced glass plate from which the elements are cut. The glass elements are shaped to concave or convex forms by a curve generator machine that is a first-step grinder. To reach the specifications for its shape, a lens goes through a sequence of processes in which it is ground by polishing particles in water. The polishing particles become smaller in each step as the lens is refined. Curve generation and subsequent grinding vary in speed depending on the frailty, softness, and oxidation properties of the optical materials. After grinding and polishing, the elements are centered so that the outer edge of the lens is perfect in circumference relative to the centerline or optical axis of the lens. Lenses made of plastic or bonded glass and resin are also produced by the same processes. Bonded materials are used to make lenses with non-spherical surfaces, and these lenses are called "hybrid asphericts". The aspherical surfaces of these lenses are completed during centering. (Holmes, 1996)

After completing the process of developing specific lenses, lenses are coated for getting protected from oxidation, to prevent reflections, and to meet requirements for "designed spectrum transmission" or color balance and rendition. The lens surfaces are carefully cleaned before coating. Techniques for applying coatings and the coatings themselves are very important issues for developing quality product. Some types of coatings include metal oxides, light-alloy fluorides, and layers of quartz that are applied to lenses and mirrors by a vacuum process. Several layers of coating may be applied for the best color and light transmission, but excessive coating can reduce the light that passes through the lens and limit its usefulness. The barrel of the ready lens includes the chassis that supports the various lens elements and the cosmetic exterior. Metal mounts, grooves, and moving portions of the lens are critical to the performance of the lens, and are machined to very specific tolerances. Lens mounts may be made of brass, aluminum, or plastic. Most metal barrel components are die-cast and machined. Metal mounts last longer, maintain their dimensions, can be machined more precisely, and can be dismantled to replace elements, if necessary. Plastic mounts are less expensive and of lighter weight. If the barrel is made of engineering plastic, it is produced by a highly efficient and precise method of injection molding. The interior surfaces of the barrel are also coated to protect them and to prevent internal reflection and flare. (Holmes, 1996)

Other parts of the lens, such as the diaphragm and auto focus module, are produced as subassemblies. The iris diaphragm is constructed of curved leaves cut out of thin sheets of metal. The metal leaves are held in place by two plates. One plate is fixed, the other moves, and has slots for sliding pins. These slide the leaves back toward the barrel to open the diaphragm or into the center to close the opening as the f-stop ring is turned. The diaphragm assembly is fastened into place when the lens mount is attached to the end of the barrel. The auto focus is also added, the optical elements are positioned, and the lens is sealed. After final assembly, the lens is adjusted and inspected rigorously. It must meet the design standards for optical resolution, mechanical function, and auto focus response. Lenses may also be tested by subjecting them to shocks, dropping, and vibration.

For developing quality lenses some of the manufacturers use full automation including industrial robots to make their products, others use large assembly lines, and still others pride themselves on hand-crafting. Quality and precision are essential to lens production, however, regardless of manufacturing approach. Incoming materials and components are rigorously inspected for quality and compliance with engineering specifications. Automated processes are also inspected constantly and subjected to tolerance checks. Quality control and stress tests are incorporated in each manufacturing step, and elements and components are measured with precise instruments. Some measuring devices are laser-controlled and can detect deviations of less than 0.0001-millimeter in a lens surface or in lens centering.

CAMERA BATTERIES

Battery is one of the most important accessories of any digital camera. The quality of battery reflects that up to what extend that will support the camera. A good battery not only provides a long backup duration but also it can support the flash of the camera for more nimber of clicks.

TYPES OF BATTERIES

There are different types of camera batteries. The batteries differ in size, type and capacity. The most common batteries are as follows:

Alkaline Disposable Battery

This battery is the most common and traditional. It mainly comes in AA and AAA sizes and can be disposed. The name "alkaline" is given to the battery since it has a potassium hydroxide alkaline electrolyte. Alkaline battery is known by its name because it is based on alkaline electrolyte of potassium hydroxide, instead of acidic ammonium chloride or zinc chloride electrolyte of zinc-carbon batteries. Other battery types also use alkaline electrolytes, but normally they use different active materials for the electrodes.

Source : website of ehow (2011)

Alkaline Rechargeable Battery

This type is one of the most popular recharable camera batteries and come in different sizes. Unlike other batteries these can be recharged and can retain their charge for years.

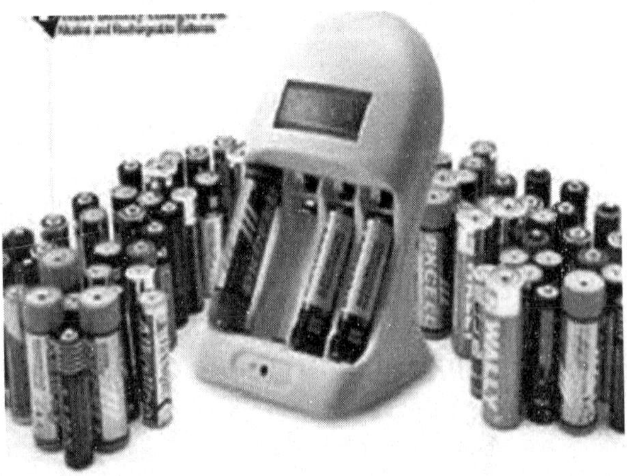

Source : website of internetsiao (2011)

NiCd (Nickel Cadmium) Battery

These are secondary cells developed on the alkaline chemistry with almost double energy density of lead acid batteries. This energy storage technology was invented in the year 1899. At that time nickel hydroxide Ni(OH)2 was used as positive electrode (cathode) and cadmium Cd was used as the negative electrode (anode), while alkaline potassium hydroxide KOH was taken as electrolyte. The small size and high rate of discharge capacity of these batteries made it a portable and popular tool of this industry. The sealed cove of these cells and the use of recombinant system made them capable of preventing electrolyte loss and finally it was helpful in extending the life of the battery.

Source : **homepage of megabatteries (2011)**

Lithium Battery

These types of batteries are used normally in our daily activities through flashlights, mobile phones, cameras and laptops etc. This type of battery is priced higher than the Alkaline AA battery and performs well even in cold weather. The lifespan of these batteries is also longer than the Alkaline AA battery and is popular in the community of photographers. However, one should ensure him/her first that the device like camera is compatible with this battery type. These battery types are most popular among all of the rechargeable battery types for portable electronic gadgets. The popularity of this type of battery is due to it's the best energy densities, no memory effect and a slow loss of charge when the gadget is not in use. Now- a-days this type of battery is achieving popularity among military and aerospace applications.

Source : **homepage of ecotech (2011)**

NiMH (Nickel Metal Hydride) Battery

Nickel Metal Hydride battery is an affordable long lasting rechargeable battery. The main downside of this type of battery is that it loses its charge when it is not in use. While using this battery it is essential recharge it before its use. NiCad and NiMH batteries are amongst the hardest batteries to charge, these batteries take more time in complete charging. While lithium ion and lead acid batteries, one can control overcharge by setting a maximum charge voltage. The nickel based battery does not has a "float charge" voltage. The charging of these batteries is based on the forcing current through the battery. The voltage to do this is not fixed in stone like it is for the other batteries. This problem makes these cells and batteries difficult to charge in parallel. Due to this vary reason one can't be assured that each cell or pack is of same resistance, and so some cells will take more current than others even when they are full. Therefore, we require a separate charging circuit for each string in a parallel pack, or balance the current in some other way.

Source : **Homepage of power 2000 batteries (2011)**

REFERENCE

Edward Holmes: An Age Of Cameras (1978)

http://www.tlr-cameras.com/Japanese/slides/Koni-Omegaflex.html

http://instructables.com (Accessed on 03-11-2011)

http://sheldonbrown.com (Accessed on 03-11-2011)

http:// 3dmodelfree.com (Accessed on 03-11-2011)

http:// ehow.com (Accessed on 03-11-2011)

http:// internetsiao.com (Accessed on 03-11-2011)

http:// megabatteries.com (Accessed on 03-11-2011)

http:// ecotechninja.com (Accessed on 03-11-2011)

http:// ngureco.hubpages.com (Accessed on 03-11-2011)

http://en.wikipedia.org (Accessed on 03-11-2011)

http://answers.com (Accessed on 03-11-2011)

Introduction to digitization tools. Lia, Jua (2001)A course in digital libraries by Yerkley, A.N. and Joirgensin, C., Vol.16 no.1, pp.31-9

Spec Kit 214 Digitizing technology for preservation. ARL, 1996

Logoze, Carl & Fielding, David, (1998), Defining collections in distributed digital libraries, D-Lib Magzine, Nov 1998. http://www.dlib.org/dlib/ november98/lagoze/11lagoze.html (Accessed on 10/08/11)

Green Spun, Philip (1997). Building a Digital SLR System. Photo.net. http://www.encyclopedia.com/topic/Cameras.aspx#1-1G2:2896600030-full (Accessed on 23/11/10)

Holmes , Gillian (1996). Camera Lens : How products are made. Encyclopedia.com. (Accessed on 18/11/10)

Holmes, Gillian (1996). Gale's How products are made: How is a camera lens made? Answers.com. (Accessed on 18/11/10)

http://en.wikipedia.org/wiki/Twin-lens_reflex_camera

4

Digital Content Management Suites

DIGITAL FILE MANAGEMENT SYSTEMS DSPACE

Hewlett-Packard Company (HP) awarded $1.8 million in March 2000 to MIT Libraries for an 18-month collaboration to build digital library software, DSpace, a dynamic repository for the intellectual output in digital formats of multi-disciplinary research organizations. HP Labs and MIT Libraries released the system worldwide in the year 2002, under the terms of the BSD open source license, one month after its introduction as a new service of the MIT Libraries. As an open source system, DSpace is now freely available to other institutions to run as is, or to modify and extend as they require for meeting local needs. From the outset, HP and MIT designed the system to be run by institutions other than MIT, and to support federation among its adopters, in both the technical and the social sense. (Smith, 2003)

DSpace preserves and enables easy access to all types of digital information. This may include text, images, moving images and data sets. Being an open source software, it is supported by an ever-growing community of developers. This team of developers is committed for continuous expansion and improvement in the software.

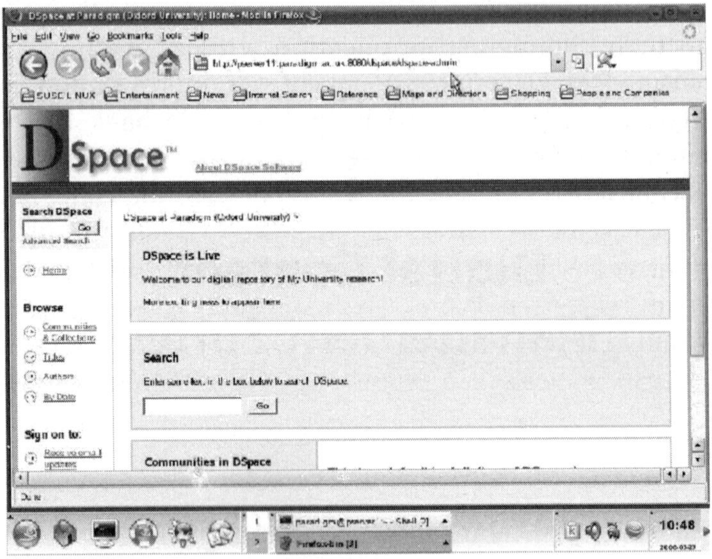

Fig. Dspace home Page

WIDER ACCESSEBILITY OF DSPACE

Largest community of users and developers worldwide

DSpace has over 900 organizations that are currently using the DSpace software in a production or project environment. The most common use is by research libraries as an institutional repository, however there are many organizations using the software to host and manage subject based repositories, dataset repositories or media based repositories. A census of Institutional Repositories in the United States was done by CLIR in 2007 and found that DSpace was the preferred Institutional Repository system software of the 446 participants in the survey.

Free open source software

The DSpace open source platform is available for free to anyone and can be downloaded from the sourceforge open source software repository. The code is currently licensed under the BSD open source license. This means that any organization can use, modify, and even integrate the code into their commercial application without paying any licensing fees. Of course, we hope if you improve upon the software, you will contribute that code back to the community for everyone's benefit. Today there are more than 100 contributors around the world contributing code, bug fixes, etc. DSpace software is managed by a smaller group of volunteer developers (called committers) that work together to plan releases and integrate new features and bug fixes submitted by the community. See our DSpace Contributor Listing for a full list of all known contributors to the platform.

Completely customizable to fit your needs

Some of the key ways you can customize the DSpace application to suit your needs are as follows:

Ability to customize or theme the user interface : You can fully customize the look and feel of your DSpace website so it will integrate seamlessly with your own institution's website and can be more intuitive for your users. DSpace provides two main user interface options: the traditional (JSP-based) interface, and Manakin (XML-based) which provides various "themes" out of the box.

Ability to customize the metadata : Dublin core is the default metadata format within the DSpace application, however you can add or change any field to customize it for you application. DSpace currently supports any non hierarchical, flat name space. However, it is possible to ingest other hierarchical metadata schemas into DSpace such as MARC and MODS. This requires using tools such as crosswalk and having some technical capability to map the transfer of data.

Standards compatible : DSpace complies with many standard protocols for access, ingest, and export. The standards DSpace supports include: OAI-PMH, OAI-ORE,

SWORD, WebDAV, OpenSearch, OpenURL, RSS, ATOM

Ability to configure Browse and Search : You can decide what fields you would like to display for browsing, such as author, title, date etc. on your DSpace website. You can also select any metadata fields you would like included in the search interface. All of the text within a given item and metadata associated with the item, are indexed for full text search if desired.

Ability to use local Authentication mechanisms : DSpace comes with plugins for most university authentication methods, including: LDAP (and hierarchical LDAP), Shibboleth, X.509, IP-based. In addition, DSpace comes with its own internal authentication method, or can be configured to use multiple authentication methods at once. You can also build your own authentication plugin if you use a custom authentication mechanism.

Configurable database : You can choose either PostgreSQL or Oracle for the database where DSpace manages its metadata.

Ability to choose the default language : The DSpace web application is available in over twenty languages. So if English is not your local language, you can customize the language which DSpace uses. Youcan alsoconfigure DSpace to supportmultiple languages, so that the language your user sees is the 'preferred language' set in their web browser.

Can manage and preserve all types of digital content

The DSpace application can recognize and manage a large number of file format and mime types. Some of the most common formats currently managed within the DSpace environment are PDF, Word, JPEG, MPEG, TIFF files. It's worth noting that, although out-of-the-box DSpace only auto-recognizes common file formats, files of any format can be managed by DSpace. DSpace also provides a simple file format registry where you can register any unrecognized format, so that it can be identified in the future.

APPLICATIONS OF DSPACE

DSpace is being used by plenty of institutions in India and abroad. Some of the screenshots of LDL (Librarians Digital Library) developed by DRTC, Bangalore {https://drtc.isibang.ac.in/ (Accessed on 03-11-2011)} are:

1. End-user interface

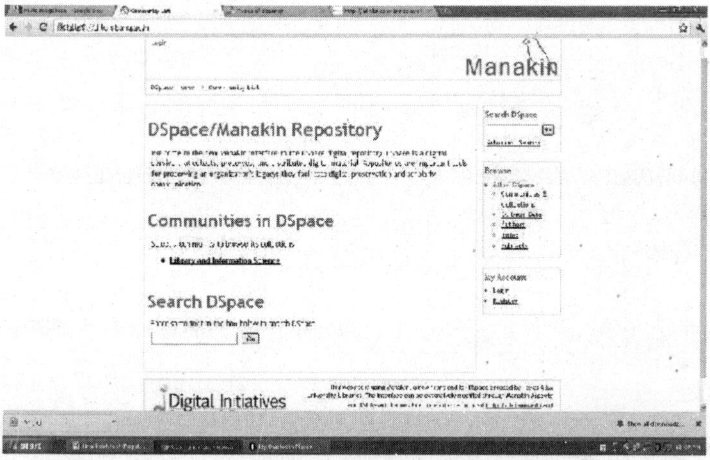

2. The user feeds his query into the search box.

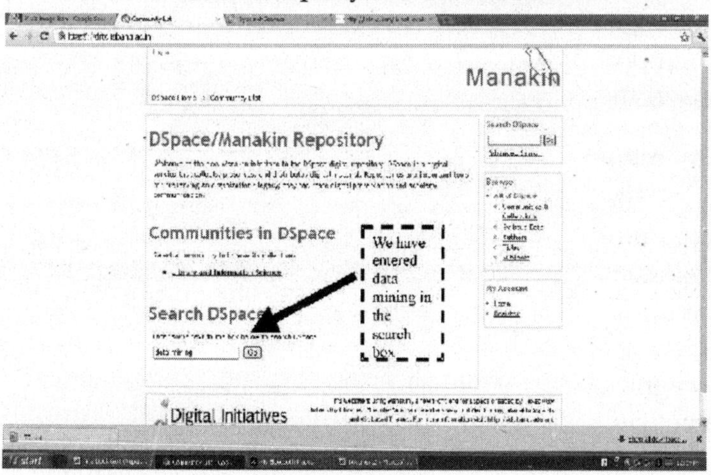

3. The output

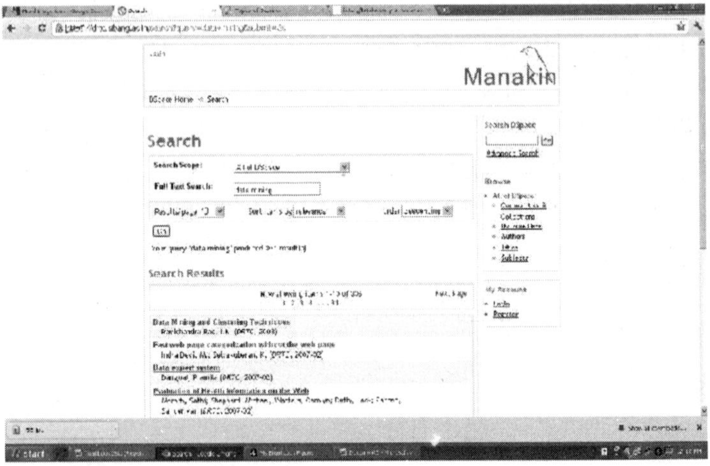

4. Out of the search results we select the document relevant to our needs.

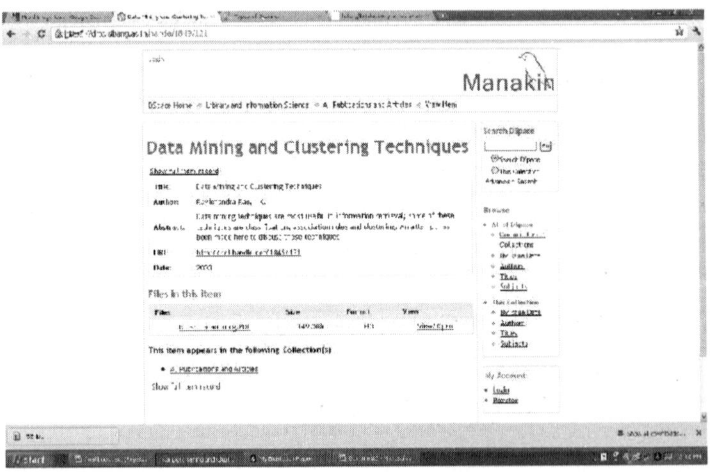

5. The document

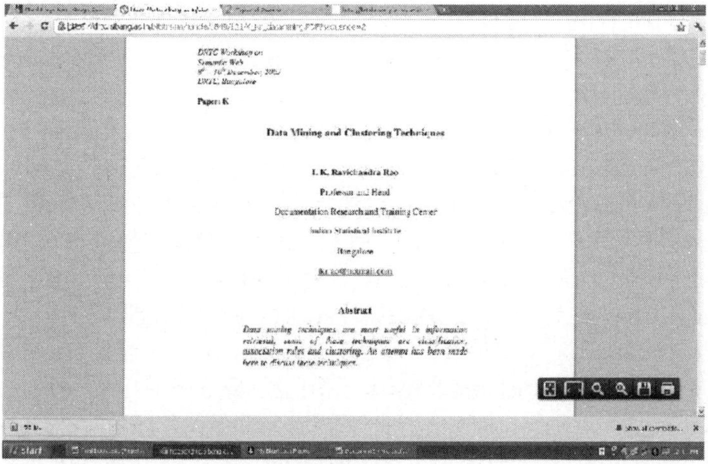

GREENSTONE DIGITAL LIBRARY

Greenstone Digital Library Software is issued under the terms of the GNU General Public License. It originated in 1996 (Witten et al., 1996), and the current production version (Greenstone2) was designed about seven years ago, although it is continually being extended. A complete redesign and reimplementation, Greenstone3, has been described (Bainbridge, 2004) and released, informed by experience with the current system and the problems and challenges faced by users, international collection developers, and practicing librarians. Greenstone3 allows documents to be dynamically added to collections; provides more flexible ways to dynamically configure the run-time system by adding new services; lowers the overhead incurred by collection developers when accessing this flexibility to organize and present their content; and modularizes the internal structure. The design is based on widely accepted standards that were unavailable when Greenstone2 was designed.

The Greenstone digital library software is a comprehensive suite of software for building and distributing digital library collections (Witten and Bainbridge, 2003). It provides a new way of organizing information and publishing it on the Internet or on removable media (e.g. CD-ROM/DVD). It is widely used in a large number of countries: see www.greenstone.org for a representative selection of example sites. Greenstone is produced by the New Zealand Digital Library Project at the University of Waikato, and distributed as open source, multilingual software in cooperation with UNESCO and the Human Info NGO. The dissemination of educational, scientific and cultural information, and particularly its availability in developing countries, is central to UNESCO's goals, and appropriate, accessible technology such as Greenstone is seen as a vital tool in this context.

Greenstone aims to enable users, particularly in universities, libraries, and other public service institutions throughout the world, to build their own digital library collections in the fields of education, science and culture. UNESCO hopes this will encourage the effective deployment of digital libraries to share information and, where appropriate, place it in the public domain. The key points that Greenstone makes it its core business to support include: design and construction of collections; distributed on the web and/or removable media;. customized structure depending on available metadata; end-user collection-building interface for librarians; reader and librarian interfaces in many languages; and . multiplatform operation.

Functionality with Librarian's Interface

The Librarian interface supports six basic activities, which can be interleaved but are normally undertaken in this order:

- If required, download any documents from the web

that need to be included in the collection. This optional step is only relevant when the collection will contain material that is sourced from the web.

- Bring documents into a collection – whether to populate a new collection or update an existing one. Metadata files may also be brought in. Users browse the computer's file space to find documents to include, and drag and drop them into place. Any documents imported from existing Greenstone collections come with existing metadata attached.
- Enrich the documents by adding metadata to them manually. Documents can be grouped into folders (it is easy to retain existing folder structures when inherited by all documents nested within them.
- Design the collection by determining its appearance and the access facility that it will support: full-text search indexes, browsing structures, the format of items on the pages that Greenstone generates, etc. This design facility is not available at the Assistant Librarian user level.
- Build the collection using Greenstone. This work is done by the computer; users are presented with a progress bar. This is the point where Expert users might examine the output of Perl scripts, which are presented in a scrolling window, to determine if anything is going wrong.
- Pass the newly-created collection to the Greenstone digital library server for previewing. The collection is automatically installed as one of those in the user's personal digital library, and a web page is opened showing the collection's home page.

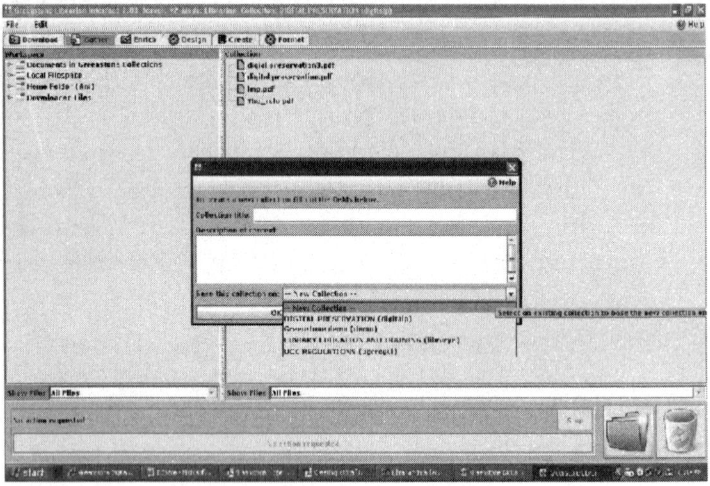

Fig. 1. Building a new collection

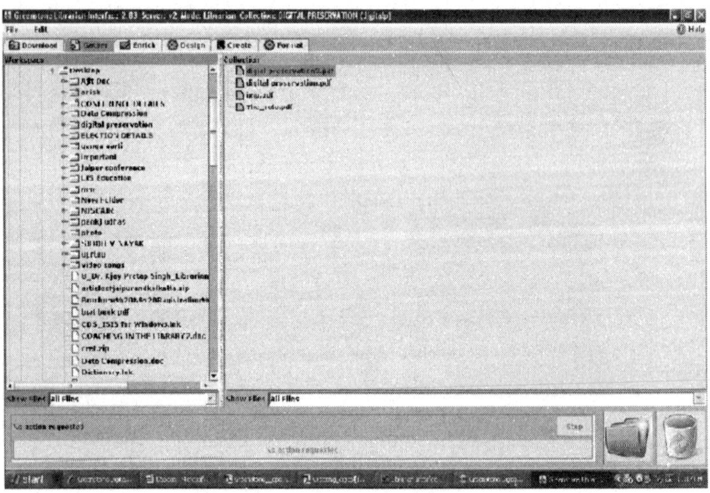

Fig. 2. Exploring the local file space

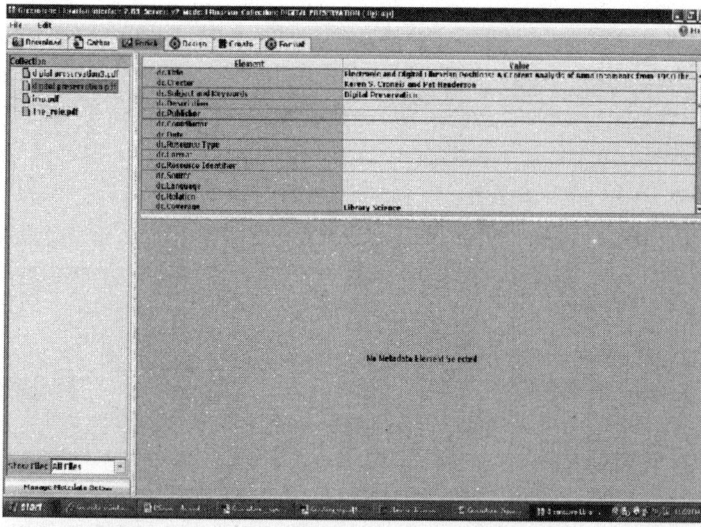

Fig. 3. Assigning metadata using the Enrich view

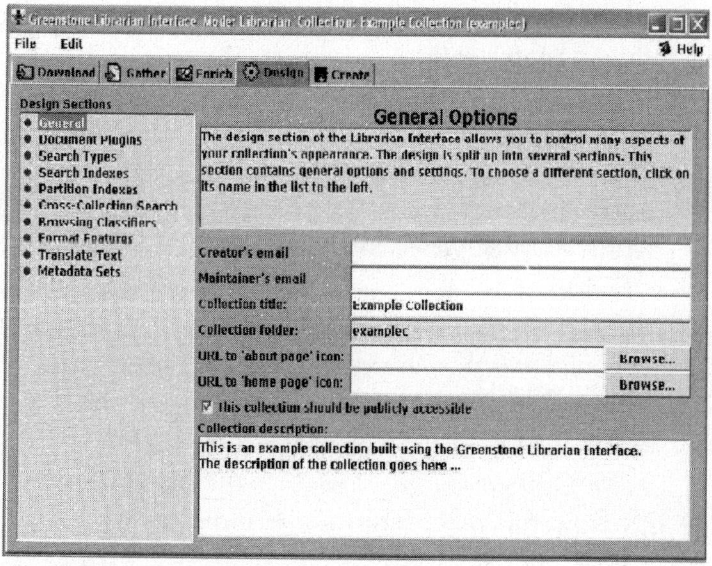

Fig. 4. Designing the collection

DIENST SOFTWARE

The NCSTRL (Networked Computer Science Technical

Reference Library) collection currently provides access to over 24,000 computer science research reports from over 120 institutions. Discovery of documents and access to those documents involve the interoperation of over forty servers communicating via the Dienst protocol and proxy servers operating through FTP and HTTP.

The collections of NCSTRL are divided into several types of *publishing authorities*. Each publishing authority has control over addition and administration of documents in their own sub-collection repositories. The metadata fields (e.g., title, author, abstract) for each document in these repositories are then indexed by one or more index servers. The metadata is accessed through Dienst protocol requests to the respective repository. The Dienst collection service allows the federation of these index and repository servers into a single uniform collection. The Dienst protocol requests [DIENST] defined for the collection service give access to the following information:

- *The list of publishing authorities that are part of the collection.* These are the organizations and repositories that are members of NCSTRL (*e.g.*, Cornell Computer Science Department, ***D-Lib Magazine***, the CoRR artificial intelligence collection).
- *The network location.* The address and port of the Dienst index servers that store indexing information for each organization. For example, indexing information for Cornell Computer Science may be stored at foo.ncstrl.org port 80 and bar.ncstrl.org port 8083.
- *Meta information about each of the index servers.* At present, this meta-information indicates whether the index server should be considered primary or secondary. However, our intention is to expand this meta-information to include data about last update of the index and performance information that could be used for performance-based query routing.

- *The correspondence of index servers to repository servers.* This provides the index servers with information on the repository servers from which they should download meta information for indexing.

Within NCSTRL, information from the collection service is used by user interface gateways to the collection. Each user interface service is configured with the host and port number of a collection server. Periodically (every hour) each user interface gateway contacts a collection server to obtain collection information, as described above. The requesting user interface server then stores the collection information internally in a table. The user interface gateway then stores this information to later create a search interface, for example showing a list of publishing authorities from which a user may choose those to which searches should be restricted, and determine to which index servers searches should be routed.

Figure illustrates the interaction between a collection server, user interface servers, and index servers in Dienst. As shown, each user interface servers queries the collection server (via protocol) for collection information. For a specific query, an individual user interface (labeled UI_1 in the figure) uses this collection information to determine which index servers should process the query.

The Dienst collection criteria are hard-wired into the implementation. NCSTRL collection is partitioned into sub-collections that correspond to the partitioning of the name space for documents in NCSTRL (i.e., each sub-collection corresponds to a Handle System naming authority). Second, the Dienst protocol and server implementation limits the ability of user interface servers to interact with more than one collection (and its associated set of sub-collections). This has prevented us from expanding the NCSTRL service to include additional scholarly collections; for example, physics, mathematics, etc. Finally, the Dienst architecture incorrectly conflates the functions of the user interface service with query routing. Although the collection service provides information for query routing, the actual dispatch of queries to index servers takes place in the user interface service. This limits our capacity to performing query routing that is highly collection.

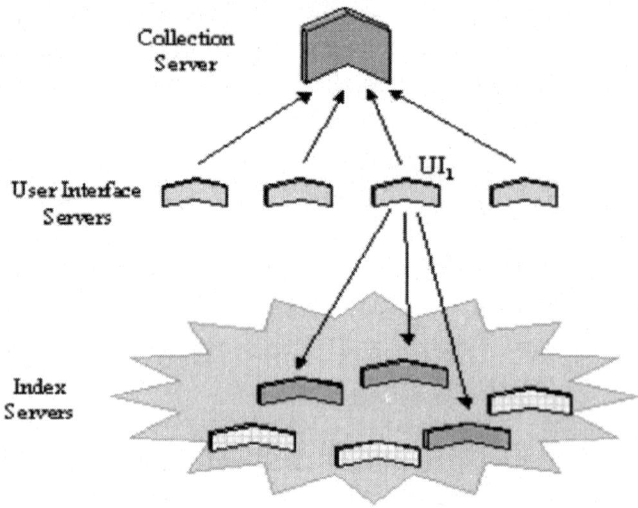

Fig. 5. Interaction between collection service and other Dienst services

- Installation of the library management service requires the ImageMagick Image Processing and Display Package and the PerlMagick Perl interface to that package.
- Installation of the index service requires a search engine able to process fielded queries and return ranked results. The Dienst implementation is configured to use freeWAIS-sf.

Modules

The Dienst software consists of a set of service modules that correspond to the services defined in the Dienst protocol.

Running the Dienst server entails supporting one or more of these service modules on a server that runs in conjunction with an HTTP server. A Dienst digital library consists of a set of these services (either running on a single server/host or distributed servers/hosts) that interoperate through the Dienst protocol.

The operational semantics of each of the services are described in the protocol document. A brief description of the implementation of each service in the software distribution is as follows:

Repository : Supports the storage of digital objects in multiple formats and versions in a file system hierarchy. The set of formats available for digital objects are customizable by the administrator. Supports access to these digital objects through the verbs defined in the repository protocol. Supports the translation (either on demand or at submission time) of input document formats to other formats (using the ImageMagick library).

Library Management : Supports the submission, withdrawal, and replacement of documents from repositories.

Index : Supports the indexing of metadata harvested from distributed repositories into the freeWAIS search engine. Supports the translation of Dienst search queries into requests to the freeWAIS search engine and formatting of responses into the Dienst response format (defined by the protocol).

Query Mediator : Supports the dispatching of queries (submitted via protocol) to multiple index servers and merging of the responses from those index servers.

Collection : Supplies the information necessary for the coordination of multiple Dienst services. This information is used by Dienst services for dispatching of service requests such as query routing by query mediators to index servers and document requests from user interfaces to repositories.

Registration : Supports the storage and access of user information for authors and users of Dienst digital libraries.

Subscription : Supports the storage of and execution of persistent queries (subscriptions) on a Dienst collection.

Browsing : Supports the construction of browsing indexes and the actual browsing of those indexes on library contents.

User Interface : Provides the human friendly front-end (HTML pages) that above services.

Some of the popular libraries which are successfully using Dienst digital library software are:

- The OpenArchives Initiative.
- NCSTRL, the Networked Computer Science Technical Reference Library.
- CoRR, the Computing Research Repository.
- Cornell University Library Making of America Collection
- ETRDL, the ERCIM Technical Reference Digital Library.
- Hein online Retrospective Law Journals
- Cornell University Library Historical Math Book Collection

Application of DIENST software at Cornell University Library Historical Math Book Collection

{http://digital.library.cornell.edu/m/math/ (Accessed on 03-11-2011)}

1. End-user interface

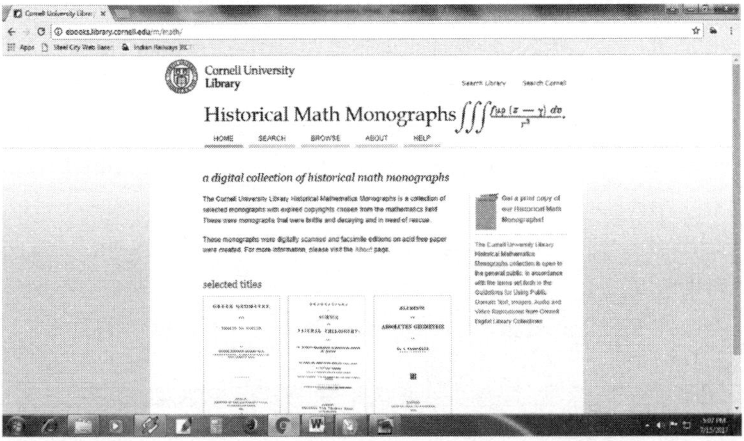

2. The user feeds his query into the search box:

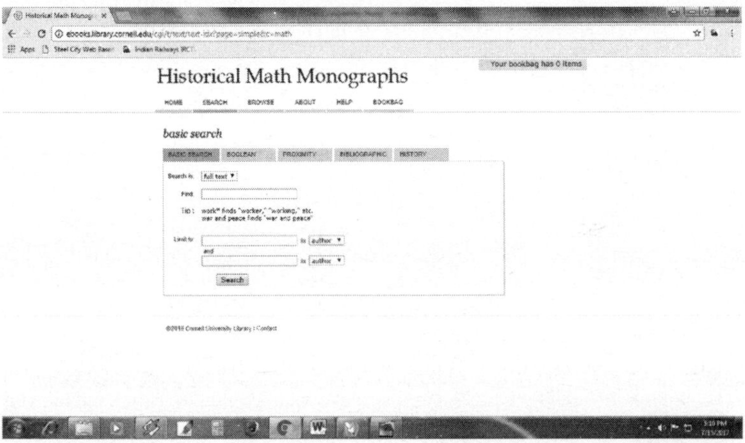

3. The output. Out of the search results we select the document relevant to our needs:

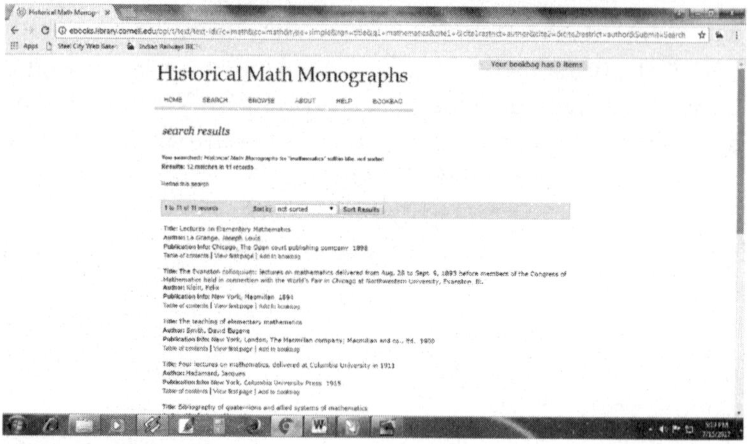

4. The document:

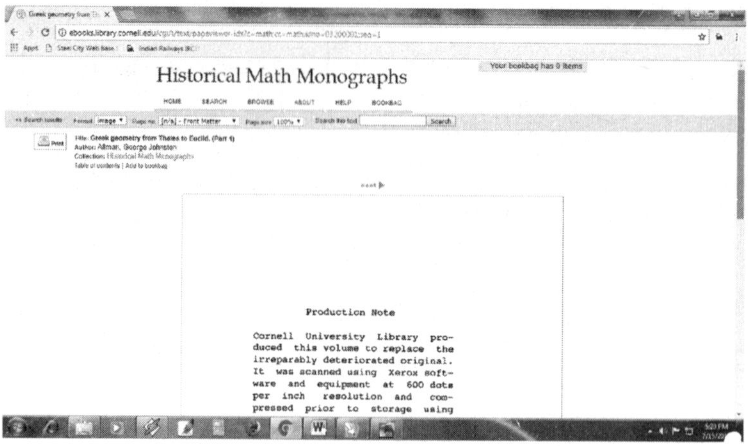

FEDORA

Fedora is an acronym for the *Flexible Extensible Digital Object Repository Architecture*. The Fedora Repository is very flexible; it is capable of serving as a digital content repository for a wide variety of uses. Fedora began in 1997 as a DARPA and NSF funded research project at Cornell University. The initial research implementation was developed by Sandra Payette, Carl Lagoze, and Naomi Dushay. Work at Cornell used a CORBA-based approach that included work on policy enforcement and extensive interoperability testing with CNRI. The first practical application of Fedora was the digital library prototype developed at University of Virginia (UVA) by Thornton Staples and Ross Wayland in 1999. The approach was redirected fit within the Web architecture and an RDBMS was added to improve performance. The UVA Fedora prototype included scalability testing for 10 million objects.

Fedora is being in use for the purpose of digital asset management and content management systems of digital documents. It provides a comfortable platform for developing institutional repositories, digital libraries and digital archives. It also supports scholarly E-publishing. The Fedora based repository can store any type of digital content, it may be in the form of videos, data sets, computer files and images etc. It can also store information in the form of metadata which provides information about the content items in any format.

The Fedora Repository is a product of Fedora Commons, a non-profit organization whose mission is to provide technology that enables durable storage and access to the digital content that increasingly records our cultural and scientific heritage. The Fedora Repository like all Fedora Commons products is provided as free, open-source software under the Apache 2.0 license.

Basic issues for the development of Fedora are as follows:

Identifiers : provision of persistent identifiers; unique names for all resources without respect for machine address.

Relationships : support for relationships between objects.

Tame Content : normalization of heterogeneous content and metadata based on an extensible object model.

Integrated Management : efficient management by

repository administrators not only of the data and metadata in a repository, but also of the supporting programs, services and tools that make presentation of that data and metadata possible.

Interoperable Access : provision of interoperable access by means of a standard protocol to information about objects and for access to object content; discovery and execution of extensible service operations for digital objects.

Scalability : provision of support for >10 million objects.

Security : provision of flexible authentication and policy enforcement.

Preservation : provision to features to support longevity and archiving, including XML serialization of objects and content versioning.

Content Recon : reuse of objects including object content being present in any number of contexts within a repository; repurposing of objects allowing dynamic content transformations to fit new presentations requirements.

Self-Actualizing Objects : ability of digital objects to disseminate launch-pads or tools for end-user interaction with content.

The digital object model offers the strengths and advantages of:

Abstraction : The object model is the same whether the object is data, behavior definitions, or behavior mechanism. It also does not matter what kind of data the digital objects is representing—text, images, maps, audio, video, geospatial data are all the same to Fedora.

Flexibility : Implementers of Fedora can design their content models to best represent their data and the presentation requirements of their specific use case.

Generic : Metadata and content are tightly linked within the digital object.

Preservation & Archiving through Fedora

Fedora's archival and preservation capabilities include:

XML : Fedora objects' XML and the schema upon which they are based are preserved at ingest, during storage, and at export.

Content Versioning : Fedora repositories offer implementers the option of versioning data objects. When a data object is versioned, the object's audit trail is updated to reflect the changes made to the object, when the change was made and by whom and a new version of the modified data is added to the object's XML. This new Datastream cascades from the original and is numbered to show the relationship between original and version. This allows users to retrieve older versions of a data object by performing a date/time search and retrieval, or the most current version if the date/time criteria are not included in the search.

Object to Object Relationships : Relationships between objects can be stored via the metadata included in the objects. This allows implementers to link together related objects into parent/child relationships.

Event History : Every object in a Fedora repository contains an audit trail, which preserves a record of every change made to the object.

A Fedora digital object consists of three parts:

1. Digital Object Identifier : A unique, persistent identifier for the digital object.

2. System Properties : A set of system-defined descriptive properties that is necessary to manage and track the object in the repository.

3. Datastream(s) : The element in a Fedora digital object that represents a content item.

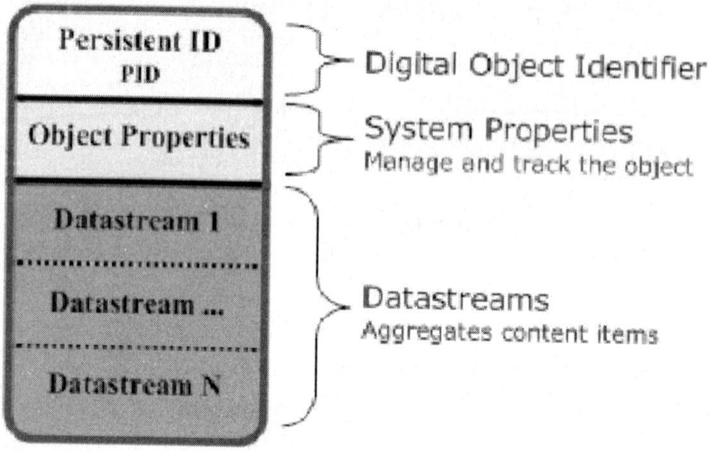

Fig. Showing the components

The basic properties that the Fedora object model defines for a Datastream are as follows:

Datastream Identifier : an identifier for the Datastream that is unique within the digital object (but not necessarily globally unique).

State : the Datastream state of Active, Inactive, or Deleted.

Created Date : the date/time that the Datastream was created (assigned by the repository service).

Modified Date : the date/time that the Datastream was modified (assigned by the repository service).

Versionable : an indicator (true/false) as to whether the repository service should version the Datastream. By default the repository versions all Datastreams.

Label : a descriptive label for the Datastream.

MIME Type : the MIME type of the Datastream (required).

Format Identifier : an optional format identifier for the Datastream. Examples of emerging schemes are PRONOM and the Global Digital Format Registry (GDRF).

Alternate Identifiers : one or more alternate identifiers for the Datastream. Such identifiers could be local identifiers or global identifiers such as Handles or DOI.

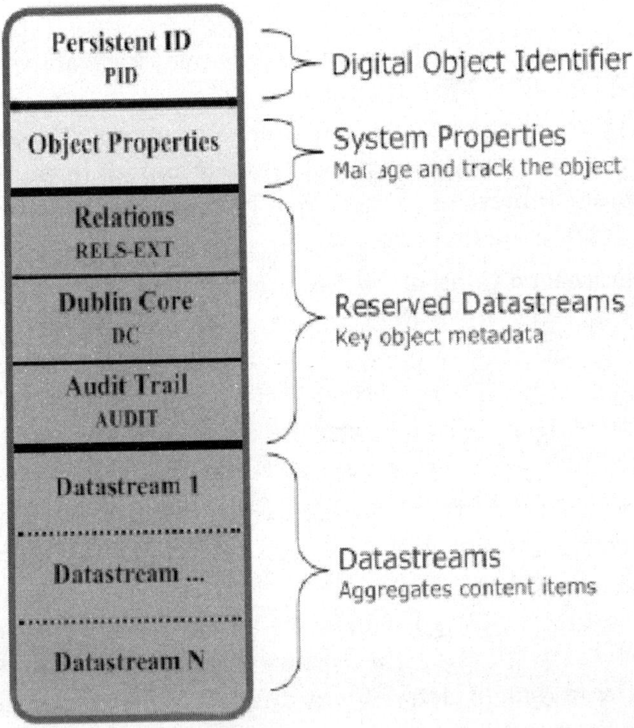

Checksum : an integrity stamp for the Datastream which can be calculale using one of many standard algorithms (MD5, SHA-1, etc.).

Bytestream Content : the "stuff" of the Datastream is about (such as a document, digital image, video, metadata record).

Aggregation : Fedora objects can refer to data that is stored locally or that is stored on any web accessible server.

Extensibility : Fedora's behavior interfaces are extensible because services are directly associated with data within a Fedora object. As the services change, the objects change along with them.

Control Group

Pertaining the the bytestream content, a new Datastream can be defined as one of four types, or control groups, as follows:

Internal XML Metadata : In this case, the Datastream will be stored as XML that is actually stored inline within the digital object XML file. The user may enter text directly into the editing window or data may imported from a file by clicking Import and selecting or browsing to the location of the XML metadata file.

Managed Content : In this case, the Datastream content will be stored in the Fedora repository and the digital object XML file will store an internal identifier to that Datastream. To get content, click Import and select or browse to the file location of the import file. Once import is complete, you will see the imported file in a preview box on the screen.

External Referenced Content : In this case, the Datastream content will be stored outside of the Fedora repository, and the digital object will store a URL to that Datastream. The Datastream is "by reference" since it is not actually stored inside the Fedora repository. While the Datastream content is stored outside of the Fedora repository, at runtime, when an access request for this type of Datastream is made, the Fedora repository will use this URL to get the content from its remote location, and the Fedora repository will mediate access to the content. This means that behind the scenes, Fedora will grab the content and stream in out the the client requesting the content as if it were served up directly by Fedora. This is a good way to create digital objects that point to distributed content, but still have the repository in charge of serving it up. To create this type of Datastream, specify the URL for the Datastream content in the Location URL text box.

Redirect Referenced Content : In this case, the

Datastream content is also stored outside the repository and the digital object points to its URL ("by-reference"). However, unlike the External Referenced Content scenario, the Redirect scenario signals the repository to redirect to the URL when access requests are made for this Datastream. This means that the Datastream will not be streamed through the Fedora repository when it is served up. This is beneficial when you want a digital object to have a Datastream that is stored and served up by some external service, and you want the repository to get out of the way when it comes time to serve the content up. A good example is when you want a Datastream to be content that is stored and served by a streaming media server. In such a case, you would want to pass control to the media server to actually stream the content to a client (e.g., video streaming), rather than have Fedora in the middle re-streaming the content out. To create a Redirect Datastream, specify the URL for the content in the Location text box.

Some of the applications of FEDORA digital library software are:

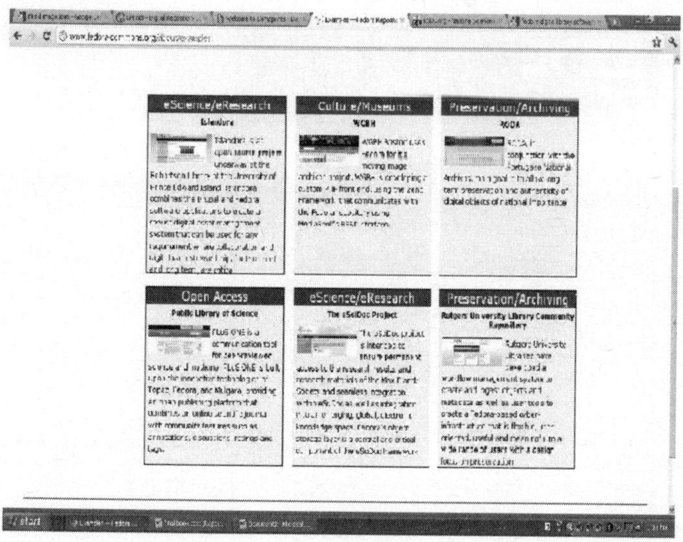

Applications of fedora digital library software in national science digital library {http://nsdl.org/ (Accessed on 03-11-2011)}

1. End-user interface:

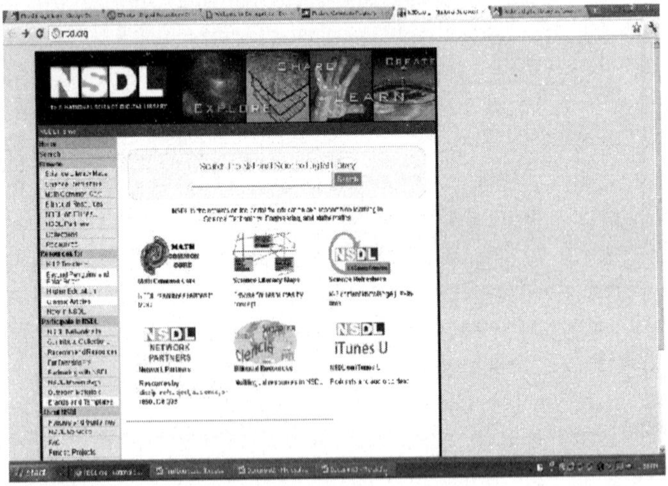

2. The user feeds his query into the search box:

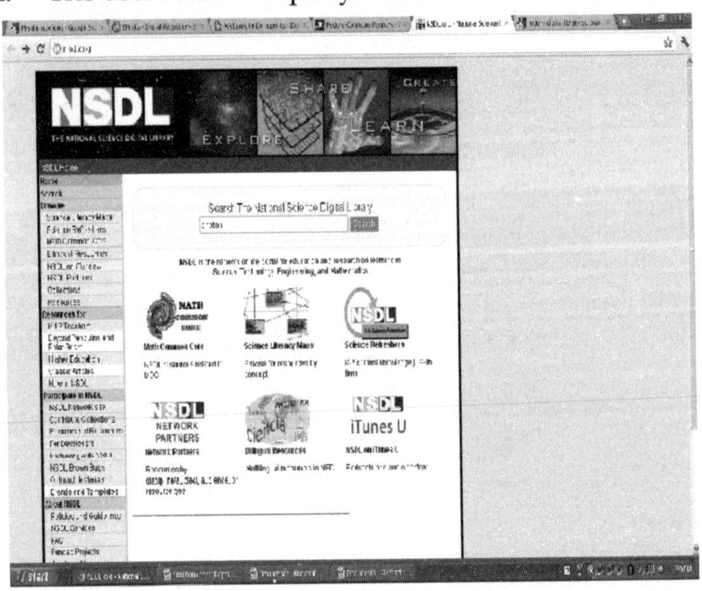

3. The output:

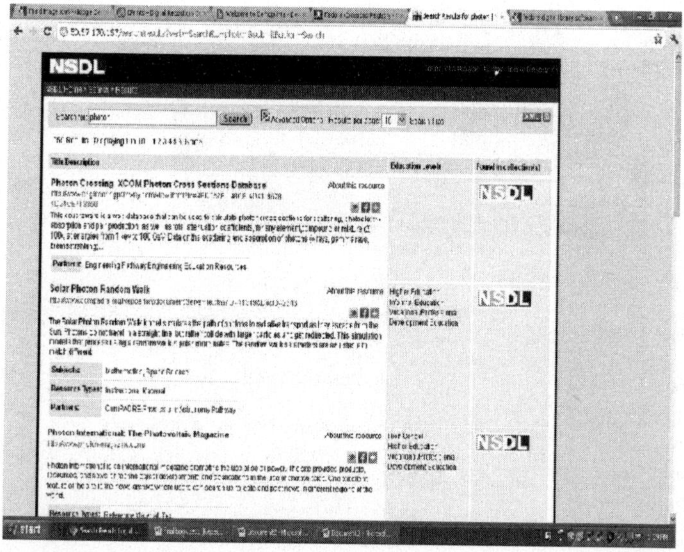

4. Out of the search results we select the document relevant to our needs:

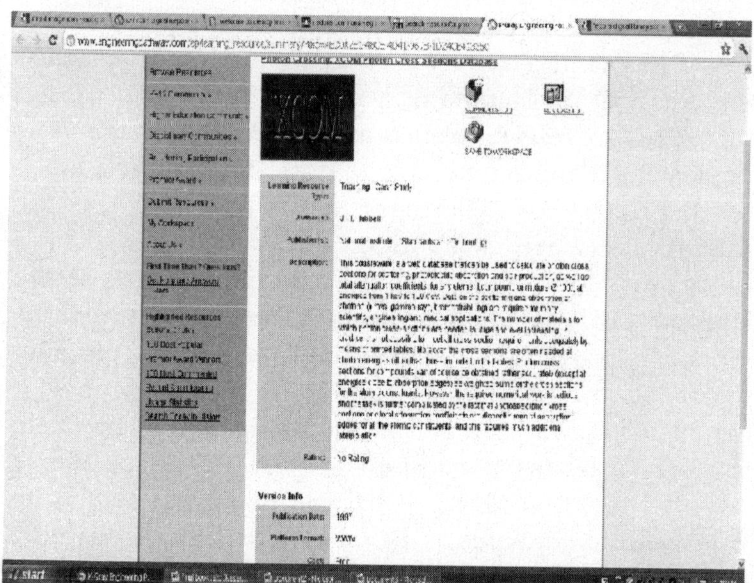

5. The document:

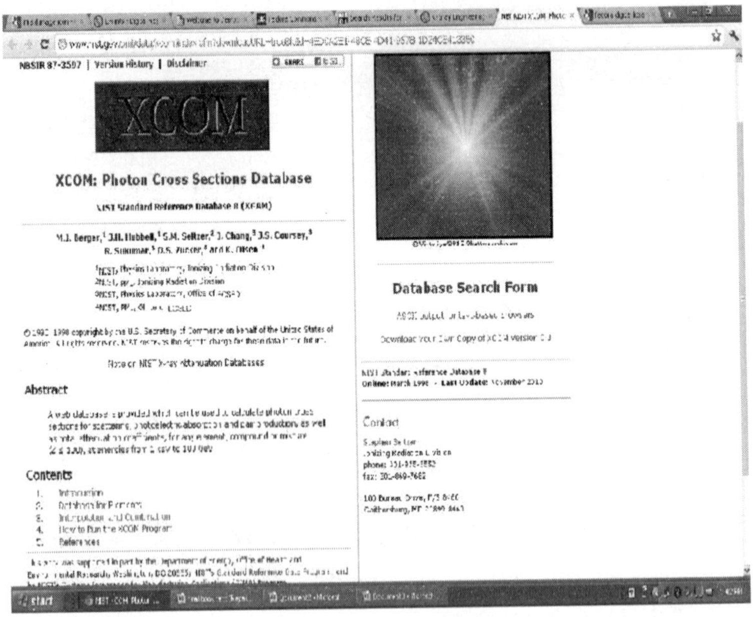

EPrints

The EPrints software package was originally designed for creating and managing open access institutional repositories of research papers and publications. It is widely implemented and is now used to store and manage a much broader range of content types and for different purposes. EPrints software is managed and developed by the Electronics and Computer Science department at the University of Southampton allows users to freely run, study, modify, improve, and release improvements of the program under the same terms. Most of the installation process is automated by way of an installation script and further help is available from the website.The default configuration is oriented towards research papers; using the system to manage different types of digital materials - such as audio archives and research data - requires changes to the configuration. EPrints is written in Perl, requires installation of the Apache web server and a number of Perl modules, and uses the MySQL database as a back-end. As with EPrints, all of this additional software is open source and freely available. It was developed under GNU/Linux and is intended to run on any UNIX-like system.There are no plans for a version to run under Microsoft Windows. Online support and advice is available from the EPrints wiki and mailing lists, although a charge is levied should implementers choose to join the EPrints community or solicit personal support services from the EPrints team. EPrints is freely distributable and, in keeping with the terms of the GPL, the source code is open and freely modifiable by programmers on the condition that modifications are also free and open.

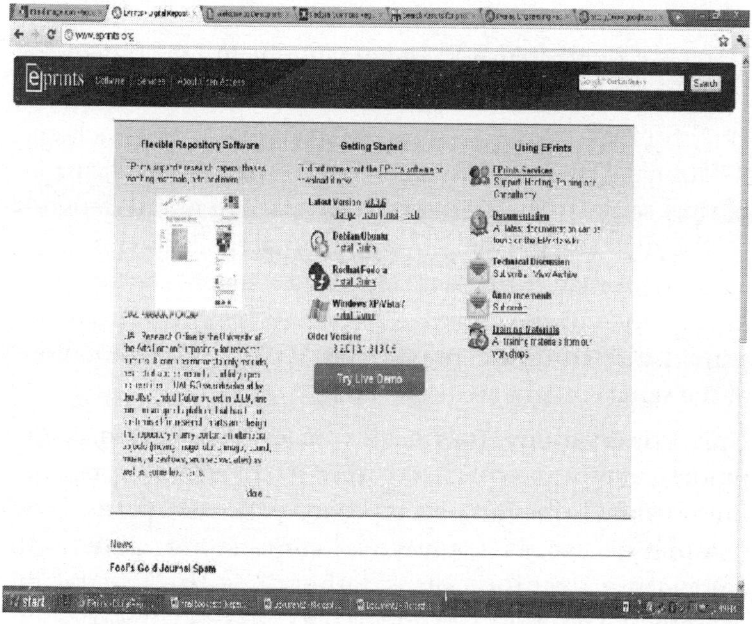

The default deposit configuration requires depositors to enter a minimum set of metadata.This set does not conform to any particular standard, although in practice, an EPrints implementation can be configured to request and store any metadata according to institutional requirements and the type of objects stored.A Dublin Core application profile for deposited ePrint items is under development as part of the JISC Digital Repositories Programme.

New objects (i.e. content file(s) + metadata) are temporarily stored in the registered user's 'workspace' until all required metadata has been entered and the object deposited: this enables depositors to put an entry 'on-hold' until all required metadata has been collected.A built-in buffer enables items to be withheld for review or approval by repository administrators before final entry into the system.This can be disabled.

Workflow : In keeping with the straightforward ingest procedures, workflow functionality is minimal. Editors and administrators can receive e-mail notification when new items are deposited and move content in and out of the submission buffer if the buffer is active.

Storage : MySQL must be installed as the back-end Relational Database Management System (RDMS) for an EPrints service. The amount of discspace required depends on the repository scale, but approximately 2MB should be allowed for each ePrint item deposited. Content can be stored in any format designed acceptable by the repository administrator during configuration. Multiple representations of the same content are acceptable.

Preservation : Functionality for long-term preservation is not currently an explicit feature of the EPrints architecture. Preservation in institutional repository software, particularly in open access, is a source of some contention, with conflicting opinions on whether it is the role of an institutional repository to undertake long-term preservation of journal and research articles that have been published elsewhere. Despite this, the EPrints team is participating in the PRESERV project to investigate and develop infrastructural digital preservation services for digital repositories.

Access : A web accessible interface enables users to search the system. Full text searching and searching on metadata fields are both possible. The software does not assume open access and can be configured to allow limited access to certain deposits or sets of deposits. The generic version of EPrints is fully interoperable with all other OAI-PMH compliant Open Archives, which means that papers in all OAI-PMH compliant Archives can be harvested using the OAI-PMH protocol.

DEMO-VERSION OF THE APLICATION OF EPRINTS DIGITAL LIBRARY SOFTWARES. {http://www.eprints.org/ (Accessed on 03-11-2011}

1. End-user interface:

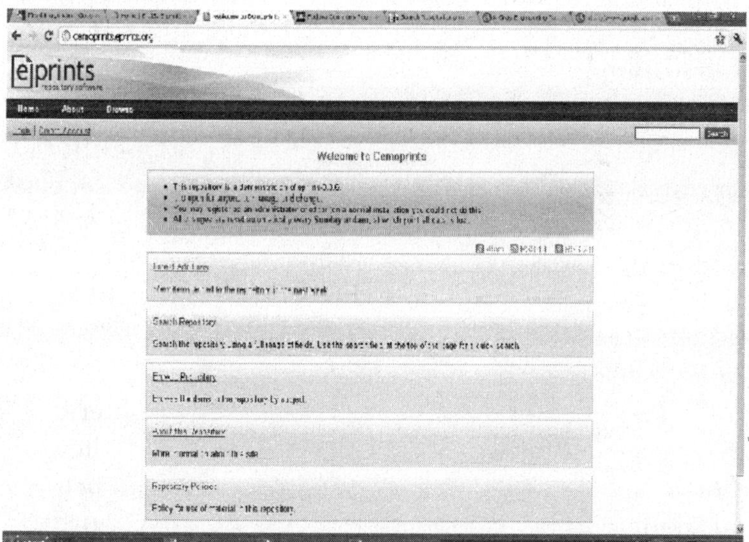

2. Select the appropriate subject from the subject directory:

3. Documents in a chosen subject directory:

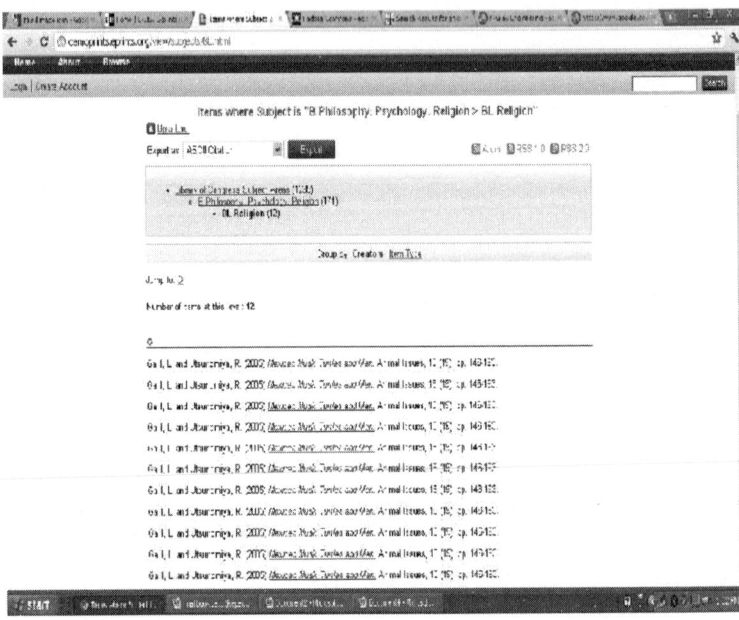

4. The document:

RESOURCE ORGANISATION AND DISCOVERY IN SUBJECT-BASED SERVICES (ROADS)

ROADS was a collaborative resource discovery development project. It was funded under the Electronic Libraries Program for designing and implementing a user-oriented resource discovery system. The result of this project was a ROADS toolkit, which is freely available and configurable kit for building information gateways. As the original ROADS project is now completed and over, the toolkit of this project is being maintained by an informal consortium of software developers who are having expertise in network-based resource identification, indexing and cataloguing. This is being done as an open-source software. ILRT is the centre which is expertise in the use of ROADS and is engaged in building several ROADS based services for varied clientele.

The software allows it user to establish and set up a **subject gateway**. On the backend, a web accessible database of records works and facilitates the search results. Records related to particular subject areas such as medicine, chemistry, technology etc enable the database for providing response of diversified queries. Each resource record consists of a number of fields like an identical URL, title, a brief description, related keywords. This gateway provide searching and browsing support with equal efficiency. The required resource can be searched through various access points in this gateway like sub-topic, sub-geography etc.

CDSware

CDSware is new software which at first existed and operated exclusively in CERN. Its creation began when Le Meur and Sanchez undertook the development one of the modules of the Library Operating System, ALEPH. After that, based on the material and the experience they obtained from they project, they continued their work by moving towards the creation of CDSware. More precisely, by the end of 1993, CERN initiated the first preprint server on the web. In 1996 this server evolved into "weblib" to give access to the whole CERN library, including books, electronic publications, and periodicals. In 2000 the "weblib" server became the CERN Document Server, which included more advanced characteristics, more functions and collections; it could run only on the website of CERN and became OAI compatible. From 1 August 2002 it has been distributed as a completed package under the brand CDSware, version 0.0.9, under the terms defined by GNU. The last version by the Development branch, v.0.1.2, was presented on 21 December 2003. The last version of the Stable branch, v.0.7.1, was released on 4 May 2005.

Characteristics and functions Technical options

Standards

OAI-PMH v.2.0.

CDSware is not compatible with Z39.50.

This program is freeware and supports the terms determined by GNU. These concern the free distribution of the software and not its price. Such software can be distributed free of charge, but CDSware charges for each service that might be requested. The code of the software is offered free of charge so that developers can modify it, change it or use some of parts to create new software that will be distributed for free. Hardware. Because of the variety of possible conditions within each organization, specific demands on CPU cannot be predicted. System demands will depend on the size of the collections, the number of users, the database platform, etc.

Software

1. *Operating system* : Linux or Solaris.
2. *Programming language* : Python and PHP.
3. *Database* : MySQL.
4. *Webserver* : Apache.
5. *Search engine* : CDSware uses its own indexing technology and a search engine designed for large data repositories.
6. *Other* : WML (website META language). ***Supported clients***. All HTML 4.0 or newer clients.

Staffing demands : Organizations will need UNIX systems administers and python programmers.

Administration of the repository and the system

Set-up. CDSware contains an automatic installation script that allows the system to be upgraded by later versions without eliminating modifications having to do with e-mail, supporting pages, or search pages.

Module-level Application Programming Interface (API). CDSware allows the programmers to modify the system's interoperability according to specific needs with the use of an API.

User registration

1. Password management : CDSware identifies multiple resources inside the system itself, users may select their own passwords (optional), CDSware offers password reminders, with a secure procedure that lets users who have forgotten their password choose a new one on their own.

2. CDSware verifies the identity of subscribed users and has other safety mechanisms. It separates authorized users who have the right to submit documents, from the rest of the system's users. It also allows the editing of user profiles.

3. CDSware restricts access according to user type, and lets the repository administrator define user access to specific content according to the level of authorization of each user (e.g. it can permit access to a repository of reports of a specific Department only by the teaching staff).

4. CDSware has multiple authentication methods that let the repository administrator define different levels of access and restrictions according to the user. Some documents might be accessible to anyone; others might be accessible to an academic community according to the IP addresses; and some others only to a restricted number of users according to their IPs/ passwords.

5. CDSware restricts access according to the level of the File/ Object. The repository administrator can restrict access to specific parts of a file.

6. CDSware manages copyright issues for documents that have been submitted to it. For each specific collection there a different copyright policy is possible. The ability to have different policies at the document level is not currently possible.

Submissions management

CDSware specifies multiple collections inside the system.

1. Those collections may be identified according to specific criteria, like subject, type of contents, aim and target group. The group of users might be academic departments, schools, etc. according to the needs of each institution. CDSware supports hierarchy within collections, as well as virtual collections (that is, it can create new virtual collections with objects from other collections).
2. CDSware defines different submission parameters for each collection. It allows the repository administrator to define different ways of submitting the documents according to their content and different review/validation parameters for each of the collections or for different user groups.
3. A special homepage for each collection can be built according to its specific needs.

Metadata

1. CDSware's basic metadata scheme is MARC21. It also supports the creation of basic Dublin Core (DC). The Open Archive Initiative (OAI) protocol additionally offers the ability to search even in non-certified DC fields (that is, additional fields not part of basic DC).
2. Since basic DC sometimes is inadequate to satisfy the needs of a specific organization, OAI supports the parallel use of metadata sets, allowing repositories to use additional metadata specifically for each specific collection.
3. So as to be more effective, metadata harvesting from individual users can be supervised, controlled, and corrected before their final distribution to the public.

4. CDSware allows the export of metadata in OAI-MARC 21 in XML.
5. CDSware lets the system administrator prevent OAI harvesting from the repository.
6. Metadata fields may be added or deleted.
7. CDSware allows the repository administrator to predefine fixed values in metadata fields to simplify their inclusion.
8. The documents retrieved by the user appear on the first screen in their simplest and most comprehensible form in HTML format. This screen, like all the others, can be formatted and can include all possible elements and in any desirable form. Additional screens present the elements of the bibliographic records in MARC21 HTML format. Bibliographic data are saved in XML MARC, but MARC HTML provides a different and more comprehensible form for the common user.
9. Support for Unicode allows the use of almost all languages.
10. Accepted content is updated and indexed in real time.

Searching abilities

The system supports:

1. full text searching (this refers to the internal searching of the system, the recovery software, and the presentation layer – not to third-party search engines);
2. truncation/wildcards (* ¼ multiple characters, ¼ one character);
3. searching in all metadata fields.;
4. searching in selected metadata fields (e.g. only in the title or the author field); and
5. browsing.
6. Google and other search engines. The HTML formats

used in the documents of CDSware can be created so as to permit searching through the web.

Cost

CDSware distribution is free under the terms of GNU. This not only means that there is no cost, but also that it can be modified and redistributed for free. It is a freeware, but that does not mean that CERN undertakes any official obligation to provide help for its technical support and installation. If a library or other organization requires help, it can be provided for a charge that is defined after a special agreement. Of course, there are electronic help lists and in practice there is easy and free support via e-mail or telephone, at least for initial installation problems. The copyright belongs to CERN.

SECURITY IN DIGITAL RIGHTS MANAGEMENT (DRM)

Security measures deployed in current DRM implementations. General requirements for security in DRM systems are explained first. Next an analysis of the security model in DRM is given. Then we take a look at various security technologies and solutions used for DRM. A DRM system requires persistent content protection, meaning that protection has to stay with the content. For example, a digital movie can be delivered securely over the Internet using standard cryptographic mechanisms.

But if the recipient can save and copy the content in an unrestricted form and put the digital copy onto the Internet, many people in the world can download the movie without reduction in quality. Therefore, the required security level in DRM systems goes beyond simply granting digital licenses to authorized users. More importantly, restrictions of the content usage rights have to be maintained after the content is delivered to the end user. Essential security requirements in DRM systems include data protection to protect against unauthorized interception and modification, unique identification of recipients to enable access control for the digital content, and effective tamper-resistant mechanism to process protected data and enforce content usage rights.

1. Cryptographic Mechanisms in Digital Right Management (DRM)

- Many DRM systems are built on various cryptographic solutions that have been studied and developed for many years. To summarize, the following subsections present some of the cryptographic primitives that are commonly used in DRM systems.

Symmetric and Asymmetric Encryption

To prevent illegal copying of digital content, the content is generally encrypted using a symmetric key algorithm. Most DRM providers keep their encryption process and algorithm details confidential. This is "security through obscurity" which is contrary to the basic Kerkhoff's Principle (Internet Solutions 2001). However, a number of companies have announced that they employ wellknown cryptographic algorithms for content encryption, such as InterTrust and MediaSnap (mediasnap.com) who say they use the Advanced Encryption Standard in their DRM solutions. Compared with standard implementations of cryptographic algorithms, nonstandard implementations of such algorithms are not as trustworthy, and probably, not as efficient (Stamp 2002). Asymmetric encryption is based on the usage of key pairs– public key and private key that are mathematically related so that data encrypted with one key can only be decrypted with the other key. The digital license containing the content decryption key must be encrypted using the public key of the receiver. Therefore, only the party holding the correct private key can decrypt the content key and get access to the content.

Digital Signatures and One-way Hash

In DRM systems, digital signatures are usually used for non-repudiable rights issuing. The clearinghouse should digitally sign licenses of the digital content. Therefore, the player application on the consumer's device can verify the correctness of the usage rights and keep the signature as a proof of rights purchase. One-way hash functions combined with digital signatures are used for integrity checking. For example, the clearinghouse uses its private key to sign the hash value of the encrypted content rights. Integrity verification of the license is through decrypting the signature using the public key of the clearinghouse and then comparing the hash value with a re-computed hash value.

WEB ARCHIVING

Web archiving is the process of collecting portions of the World Wide Web and ensuring the collection is preserved in an archive, such as an archive site, for future researchers, historians, and the public. Due to the massive size of the Web, web archivists typically employ web crawlers for automated collection. The largest web archiving organization based on a crawling approach is the Internet

Archive which strives to maintain an archive of the entire Web. National libraries, national archives and various consortia of organizations are also involved in archiving culturally important Web content. Commercial web archiving software and services are also available to organizations who need to archive their own web content for corporate heritage, regulatory, or legal purposes.

Digital Certificates

Digital certificates are used to authenticate or verify the identity of the parties involved in the system. In DRM systems, it is essential to use this mechanism to ensure that the packaged digital content is from the genuine authorized content distributor. The certificates of fake packaging applications should be revoked to limit the damage they can cause.

2. Individualization

Most current DRM solutions rely on unique identification of user devices. Each license is bound to a unique playback device, so the license stored in one device cannot be transferred or used by another device. To illustrate how this works, we use the example of the individualization process in Microsoft WMRM: An individualized Windows Media Player is one whose DRM component has been individualized, which is like receiving a security upgrade (Microsoft 2002b). Content providers may require their digital content to be played only on the player that has been individualized. During individualization process, Microsoft Individualization Service generates a unique DLL (Dynamic Library Link) that is bound to the client computer using its hardware ID6. Once the player has been individualized, a public/private key pair is generated. The private key is stored in the DLL file that is generated in the individualization process. The corresponding public key is used as the player's identifier when requesting a license and the clearinghouse will encrypt the license using this key. If the player is moved to another host, it will require individualization, because there is no corresponding DLL file binding to the new host. The license granted by the clearinghouse is not transferable or usable on another computer.

In the context of DRM, individualization can reduce the damage caused by system cracking, because if the DRM module on a user's computer is compromised, only that terminal is affected. However, it introduces another problem concerning the portability of rights: When the user wants to watch the movie at his friend's place or listen to the music on his portable devices (PDAs, mobile phones, portable players, etc.), he has to acquire new licenses for every device to enable content consumption. To reduce the impact of digital licensing process on the user experience, some DRM solutions allow users to back up their licenses and restore to another computer. To prevent abuse, users can only do this a fixed number of times.

3. Digital Watermarking

A digital watermark is an imperceptible signal that can be inserted into digital content for a variety of purposes, including captioning and copyright control. An important property of watermarks is robustness to common signal transformations such as file filtering and compression, and resistance to tampering (Cox and Miller 1997). In DRM systems, watermarks can be used for binding information to digital content, such as content owners, the buyer of the content and payment information. They should be recoverable by special watermark-reading software to check content copyright and determine royalty payments. Watermarks can also be used forensically to trace digital pirates. Many companies provide a web spider service that routinely searches the web and tests for digital files that have been watermarked. The purpose of this service is to detect violations of copyright for registered content owners. Once the copyright violation is detected, content owners will be notified and the infringer will be likely taken to court. Moreover, watermarks can be used for data annotation and access control. These watermarks are called annotation watermarks (Dittmann, Wohlmacher and Ackermann 2001).

Current watermarking technology is imperfect. There is no standard watermarking solution in real applications. The robustness of many watermarking systems is not very satisfactory. The majority of copyrights marking schemes in the literature are vulnerable to attacks (Petitcolas, Anderson, and Kuhn 1998). The current state of watermarking technology is such that if an attacker knows the watermarking technique, he can almost certainly mangle the watermark beyond recognition (Stamp 2002). It is possible for a hacker to remove the content usage restrictions and add additional usage rights for himself. Therefore, merely applying watermarking technologies to the DRM solution may not be secure enough to meet the commercial requirements.

4. Legal Issues

Here we will discuss on the current legal situation in the domain of DRM, focusing on the US Digital Millennium Copyright Act (DMCA), the US Security Systems Standards and Certification Act (SSSCA), the European Union Copyright Directive (EUCD) and the Australian Copyright Amendment (Digital Agenda) Act 2000.

Digital Millenium Copyright Act (DMCA)

The Digital Millennium Copyright Act (DMCA), passed in 1998, is an American law implementing the World Intellectual Property Organization (WIPO) Copyright Treaty and Performances and Phonograms Treaty (WIPO Treaties) (Harvard 2000). DRM is backed by the DMCA. Any attempt for the creation and distribution of DRM circumvention tools even for legal reasons may violate federal law under DMCA. Several legal cases attracting a much attention were:

- The arrest of Dmitry Sklyarov, a Moscow graduate student, for defeating a DRM system used in Adobe's eBook Reader (EFF 2001).
- The lawsuit threatened against a research team led by Professor Ed Felten for breaking a DRM system developed by the Secure Digital Media Initiative (SDMI) (Greene 2001).

- The court case against 2600.org, an open source software forum, for posting a program 'DeCSS' to decrypt the content of DVDs (Stevenson 1999). Many people claim that DMCA stifles innovation and academic freedom (ACM 2001) and is a threat to open source software development. A lot of disputes are going on whether the DMCA should be altered to guarantee free speech.

Security Systems Standards and Certification Act (SSSCA)

The Security Systems Standards and Certification Act (SSSCA) is a draft bill for a US law, being developed by Senators Fritz Hollings and Ted Stevens with the assistance of the Walt Disney Company. The bill would require hardware manufactures of any digital data processing devices such as PCs, portable music players, mobile phones, digital cameras and a lot more with a microprocessor to build in DRM functionality, including copy protection, into their products. Anyone in U.S. who produces, imports or provides digital devices without built-in DRM would be breaking the law. If the bill passes, it would not only influence hardware manufacture but also concern software applications and operating systems in America. The user is no longer allowed to modify the software running on his computer or capture the digital content on the path from storage to the screen or speakers. Moreover, it would impose a heavy burden on the manufacturers as a consequence of the additional requirement of the system. Many vendors are worried that the increased prices and the complexity of the system will drive people away from new equipments with copy protection built in.

European Union Copyright Directive (EUCD)

The European Union Copyright Directive (EUCD) is a directive for implementing the WIPO treaties in the European Union member states into national law. If the current directive were passed without modification, it would be a criminal offence to break or attempt to break the copy protection or DRM systems on digital content. The main concerns raised by the EUCD is that it could prevent teachers copying materials for their students and prohibit academic research on security issues of an operating system or a protection mechanism. In order to develop playback tools, developers would be forced to sign licenses with the creators of a format, because it is illegal for any circumvention of copyright protection mechanism. Critics argue that the EUCD is even more restrictive than US Digital Millennium Copyright Act (Leyden 2002).

Copyright Amendment (Digital Agenda) Act

In Australia, the Copyright Amendment (Digital Agenda) Act 2000 (DACA) is similar to the US Digital Millennium Copyright Act. The DACA introduces new criminal offences and civil remedies regarding the intentional removal and alteration of electronic rights management information, typically including details about the copyright owner, and terms and conditions of use of the copyright material. Manufacture, sales and dealing with unauthorized broadcast decoding devices will result in civil remedies and criminal sanctions unless such devices are for personal use. It is illegal to provide computer programs, or manufacture, sell, import or advertise devices designed to circumvent copyright protecting measures. The exceptions to this include the reproduction of computer programs to make interoperable products, to correct errors and for security testing, activities covered by libraries and archives exceptions, the use of copyright material for the Crown, and activities covered by the statutory licences for educational institutions and institutions assisting persons with a disability under Part VB of the Copyright Act.

REFERENCES

Association of Research Libraries (1995). Definition and Purpose of a Digital Library, Association of Research Libraries, Washington, DC, available at: www.ifla.org/documents/libraries/ net/art-dlib.txt (Accessed June 23, 2009).

Simon, S.J. (2008). "Information architecture for digital libraries", First Monday, Vol. 13 No. 12, available at: www.firstmonday.org/htbin/cgiwrap/bin/ojs/ index.php/fm/article/viewArticle/2183/2059 (Accessed June 10, 2009).

Cronies, K.S. and Henderson, P. (2002). "Electronic and digital librarian positions: a content analysis of announcements from 1990 through 2000", Journal of Academic Librarianship, Vol. 28 No. 4, pp. 232-7.

Stoffle, P. (2003). "Continuing to build the future: academic libraries and their challenges", Portal: Libraries and the Academy, Vol. 3 No. 3, pp. 363-80.

Borgman, C.L. (1999). "What are digital libraries? Competing visions", Information Processing & Management, Vol. 35, pp. 227-43.

Choi, Y. and Rasmussen, E. (2006). "What is needed to educate future digital librarians: a study of current practice and staffing patterns in academic and research libraries", D-Lib Magazine, Vol. 12 No. 9, available at: www.dlib.org/ dlib/september06/choi/ 09choi.html (Accessed June 14, 2009).

Carr, R. (2004). *The Challenge of e-Science for Research Libraries*. From http://www.bodley.ox.ac.uk/librarian/escience/escience.htm. (Accessed July 02, 2010).

Carlson, S. (2006). Lost in a sea of science data: librarians are called in to archive huge amounts of information, but cultural and financial barriers stand in the way. *The Chronicle of Higher Education*, 52, 35.

Lawrence, B. (2005). Function creep and institutional repositories. *Bryan's Blog*. From http://home.badc.rl.ac.uk/lawrence/blog/2005/03/31/function_creep_and_ institutional_ repositories.

Stamp, M. (2002). Digital Rights Management: The Technology Behind the Hype. Cupertino, CA. http://home.earthlink.net/~mstamp1/papers/DRMpaper.pdf. (Accessed July 02, 2010).

Cox, I.J. and Miller, M.L. (1997). A review of watermarking and the importance of perceptual modeling. Proc. of Electronic Imaging 97, February 1997. NEC Research Institute.

Dittmann, J., Wohlmacher, P. and Ackermann, R. (2001). Conditional and User Specific Access to Services and Resources using Annotation Watermarks. Communications and Multimedia Security Issues of